A JOYCEAN SCRAPBOOK

Word_well_

in association with the National Library of Ireland

A JOYCEAN SCRAPBOOK

From the National Library of Ireland

Compiled by Katherine McSharry

First published in 2004 by
Wordwell Ltd in association with the National Library of Ireland
PO Box 69, Bray, Co. Wicklow
www.wordwellbooks.com

Copyright © The National Library of Ireland

Library of Congress Cataloging-in-Publication Data are available for this book.

A CIP catalogue record for this book is available from the British Library.

ISBN 1869857 73 9 (paperback)
ISBN 1869857 74 7 (hardback)

Cover design: Rachel Dunne
Copy editing: Aisling Flood
Typesetting and layout: Wordwell Ltd
Book design: Rachel Dunne

Printed by ebrook, Dublin

CONTENTS

● **JOYCE AGED SIX-AND-A-HALF**
Courtesy of the Poetry/Rare Books Collection,
University Libraries, State University of New York
at Buffalo

FOREWORD

The National Library of Ireland has had a long association with the writer James Joyce, who immortalised his memories of the Library by including scenes set there in both *A portrait of the artist as a young man* and *Ulysses*. Over the years the Library has accumulated a substantial collection of Joyce's works, in both printed and manuscript form, including, in recent years, important collections of drafts of *Ulysses*. However, quite apart from Joyce's own works, the Library is also extremely rich in the material that illustrates the world in which James Joyce grew up and in which his novels are set. The Library holds extensive collections of period photographs, newspapers and magazines, prints and drawings, music and songsheets, posters and postcards. Extensive research has been carried out on these collections by Katherine McSharry for the purpose of the 2004 exhibition 'James Joyce and *Ulysses* at the National Library of Ireland'. Some of these images have now been gathered together by Katherine in this Joycean scrapbook, and we hope that they will give readers some insight into the world from which the genius of James Joyce emerged.

Aongus Ó hAonghusa
Acting Director
National Library of Ireland

PREFACE

James Augustine Joyce was born in Dublin on 2 February 1882. Apart from some months spent in Paris in late 1902 and early 1903, he lived for the most part in Ireland until he reached the age of 22. In June of 1904, however, he met the Galway woman with whom he would spend the rest of his life, Nora Barnacle, then working in Finn's hotel in Dublin. By October they had resolved to leave Ireland together and sailed away to make a new life in continental Europe. Thereafter, Joyce spent his life between various European cities, most notably the three that are listed after the conclusion of the final episode of *Ulysses*—Trieste, Zurich and Paris. Between his departure from Ireland with Nora at the end of 1904 and his death in 1941, Joyce returned to Dublin on only a few occasions and not at all after 1912.

The year 1904 was, therefore, a key time in the author's life, and not solely because it marked the definitive transition between his young life in Ireland and the 36 years he would live in the cities of Europe. It was also in that year that Joyce's first work as a creative writer was published; some of the short stories that later became part of the collection *Dubliners* were published in *The Irish Homestead*, and a number of Joyce's poems appeared in *Dana* and *The Venture*. This biographical separation into pre- and post-1904 has been reflected in the layout of this book, which features a selection of the images appearing in the exhibition 'James Joyce and *Ulysses* at the National Library of Ireland'. The first section focuses on Joyce's early years and offers a picture of selected aspects of the city and country in which he grew up, between 1882 and 1904. These include the popular culture of his native city, particularly music, and political events in Ireland mediated through political cartoons and ephemera. The second section of the book concentrates on material illustrating Joyce's life and works and some of the historical backdrop against which he wrote from the end of 1904 until his death in 1941 and—a little—beyond. It includes imagery relating to the complex publishing history of Joyce's work and focuses particularly on the genesis and dissemination of *Ulysses,* the novel that reflected and refracted the world of his youth.

Throughout the book, the captions accompanying the images highlight and make explicit the connections between the images presented, on the one hand, and Joyce's life and work, particularly *Ulysses*, on the other. In general, however, we have been anxious to keep the text to a minimum and to let this visual material speak for itself. We hope that this collection of eclectic, diverse, surprising and sometimes disconcerting images will add another dimension to the experience of those of you who already know Joyce's work. Just as importantly, we also hope that some of the material in this scrapbook will encourage those of you who have not yet done so to engage with the work of one of the most remarkable of writers.

ACKNOWLEDGEMENTS

All images are reproduced by permission of the Council of Trustees of the National Library of Ireland, except where otherwise indicated.

Where images are credited to other institutions, they are copyright to them and may not be reproduced without their express permission.

The assistance of the following in the production of the book is gratefully acknowledged: Hyder Abbas, Matthew Cains, Emma Costello, Luca Crispi, Catherine Fahy, Joanna Finegan, Stacey Herbert, Gerard Long, Sandra McDermott, Brian McKenna, Gráinne MacLochlainn, Hugh Murphy, Colette O'Daly, Siobhán O'Donovan, Colette O'Flaherty, Dónall Ó Luanaigh, Sara Smyth and all the other staff of the National Library who have contributed directly or indirectly, Orna Hanly, Emma Scally and Martin Spillane.

The National Library is grateful to all at Wordwell for their help in the production of this book, particularly Rachel Dunne, Aisling Flood, Andrew Gregory, Nick Maxwell and Niamh Power.

Photography by David Monahan.

● READING ROOM, NATIONAL LIBRARY OF IRELAND, c.1900.

Mr. H. ... Mouttlot ...
Mr. Fredk. Mouttlot ...

heatre Royal
and
Opera House

Part 1 HOME

HOME

James Joyce spent his childhood and adolescence in and around Dublin city and county, at a variety of addresses, reflecting the steady decline of his family's fortunes. He attended Clongowes Wood boarding school in the neighbouring county of Kildare when he was very young—starting there aged six—and later Belvedere College, both Jesuit schools. He was also among the privileged few to attend university, at the Catholic University College on St Stephen's Green, between 1898 and 1902. A selection of images illustrate these years and also serve as a reminder that Joyce, while he could be aloof and reserved, took an active part in the social life of Dublin—acting in dramatic sketches, speaking at the university Literary and Historical Society, beginning to make a name for himself as a critic and reviewer.

Much of the activity of that social world centred on music, which was extremely important to the Joyce family; Joyce himself at one time toyed with the idea of pursuing a professional singing career. The profusion of musical references in *Ulysses* (in which one of the main characters, Molly Bloom, is a concert soprano) also emphasises the importance of music for Dubliners around the turn of the last century. Some of the most colourful and vibrant images in the scrapbook illustrate aspects of this musical world, including programmes for performances mentioned in Joyce's work, images of the theatres and music halls, portraits of the performers and beautifully illustrated sheet music for the songs that Joyce, and his fictional creations, loved to sing.

Another dimension of Dublin's social and intellectual life depicted here concerns the National Library of Ireland itself, where Joyce set the 'Scylla and Charybdis' episode of *Ulysses*. When Joyce was a young man the Library was a very social, bustling place, effectively serving as the reading room of University College and catering to hundreds of readers, young and old, on a daily basis. Joyce was one of those who not only used the Reading Room for study purposes but also lingered by the colonnades outside, chatting, smoking and philosophising. A series of images capture the National Library at the time, including a portrait of the librarian, Thomas William Lyster, who, with his colleagues Richard Best and William Kirkpatrick Magee ('John Eglinton'), is fictionalised in *Ulysses*. A related set of images show some of the figures and undertakings of the Literary Revival. Many of those active in the Revival were regular readers in the Library, where the staff were sympathetic to and engaged with the Revival project.

In addition to this social and intellectual context, this first section of the book features visual material relating to two divisive areas in Irish society—politics and religion. The politics section features political cartoons and propaganda responding, often in exaggerated fashion, to some of the significant political events of Joyce's early life, including the 1882 Phoenix Park murders, the struggles for and against Home Rule, the split in the Irish Parliamentary Party and the death of Charles Stewart Parnell, a figure of enormous importance to the Joyce family. Also included is material depicting the British administration in Ireland and the anti-Semitism evident in Ireland in 1904.

Of course, *Ulysses*, perhaps more than any novel, is intimately associated with the city in which it is set. This first part of the book also depicts the Dublin places and characters known to Joyce, many of which and of whom appeared in various guises in his fiction. Combined with the other visual material, these offer us a glimpse into the world of Joyce's youth and of his fiction.

DUBLIN CITY AND SUBURBS

● **COLLEGE GREEN,** showing the Bank of Ireland (the Irish House of Parliament before the Act of Union in 1800) on the right. In the 'Lestrygonians' episode of *Ulysses* Leopold Bloom sees a flock of pigeons fly by this building and speculates about their thoughts.

Palmerston Park   Rathmines

● **PALMERSTON PARK RATHMINES,** an affluent city suburb served by Dublin's network of trams.

Custom House, Dublin.

● **THE CUSTOM HOUSE,** on the north bank of the River Liffey.

● **EDEN QUAY,** with a view of the Loopline Bridge and the Custom House in the background.

● **STRAND ROAD, SANDYMOUNT.** Stephen Dedalus wanders along Sandymount strand in the 'Proteus' episode of *Ulysses*.

● **SACKVILLE (O'CONNELL) STREET,** one of Dublin's main thoroughfares.

Sackville Street.   Dublin.

● **SACKVILLE (O'CONNELL) STREET,** with a view of Nelson's Pillar, which features in Stephen Dedalus's 'Parable of the plums'.

Dublin. Grafton Street.

● **GRAFTON STREET,** looking toward Trinity College.

● **THE PIER IN KINGSTOWN**
(now Dún Laoghaire), which
Stephen Dedalus mentions in
the 'Nestor' episode of *Ulysses*.

● **HOWTH HARBOUR,** north
County Dublin. In *Ulysses*
Leopold Bloom proposed to
Molly on Howth Head, the hill
above the harbour.

● **ST STEPHEN'S GREEN** park in Dublin city centre; Leopold Bloom remembers his daughter Milly playing here as a child.

● **PHOENIX PARK, DUBLIN,** showing the Wellington Monument. The Irish viceroy's lodge was situated in the Phoenix Park, and *Ulysses* describes the viceregal cavalcade leaving the Park and driving through Dublin city.

● **DENIS J. MAGINNI,** by 'Bay' of Dublin. Maginni (real name Maginnis) was a professor of dancing who had premises on North Great George's Street and who makes a brief but flamboyant appearance in *Ulysses*.

● **JOSEPH P. NANNETTI,** printer and politician (1851–1915), who worked for the *Freeman's Journal* and was an Irish MP and lord mayor of Dublin in 1906. He appears in the 'Aeolus' episode of *Ulysses*.

● **J.C. DOYLE,** a popular Dublin professional baritone who won the Feis Ceoil in 1899. Joyce performed in a concert with Doyle in August 1904, and the concert tour of his fictional creation Molly Bloom was to feature a duet with Doyle.

● **TOM KETTLE,** author and politician (1880–1916), who knew Joyce in University College and who died fighting in World War I.

● **PADRAIC COLUM,** author (1881–1972), by 'Bay' of Dublin. Joyce and Colum were both regular readers in the National Library of Ireland, and Colum and his wife Mary became lifelong friends of the Joyce family.

● **OLIVER ST JOHN GOGARTY,** surgeon, writer and wit (1878–1957), as a schoolboy. Gogarty, Joyce's friend and rival, was the model for the character of Malachi 'Buck' Mulligan in *Ulysses*.

FASHION

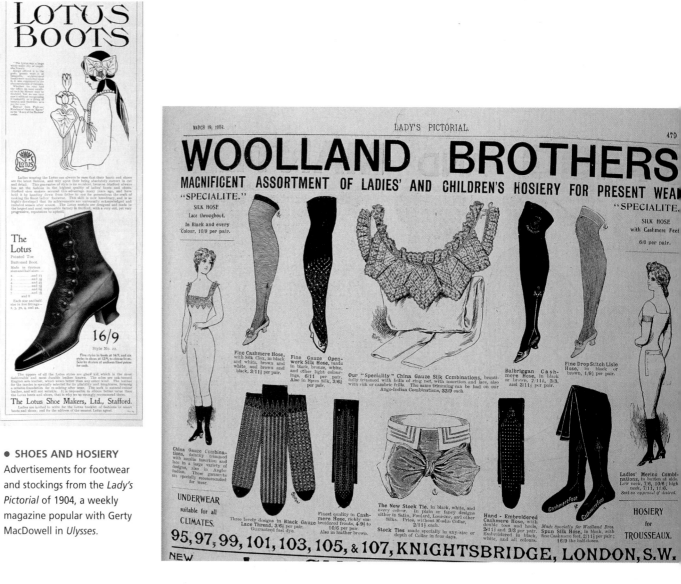

● **SHOES AND HOSIERY**
Advertisements for footwear and stockings from the *Lady's Pictorial* of 1904, a weekly magazine popular with Gerty MacDowell in *Ulysses*.

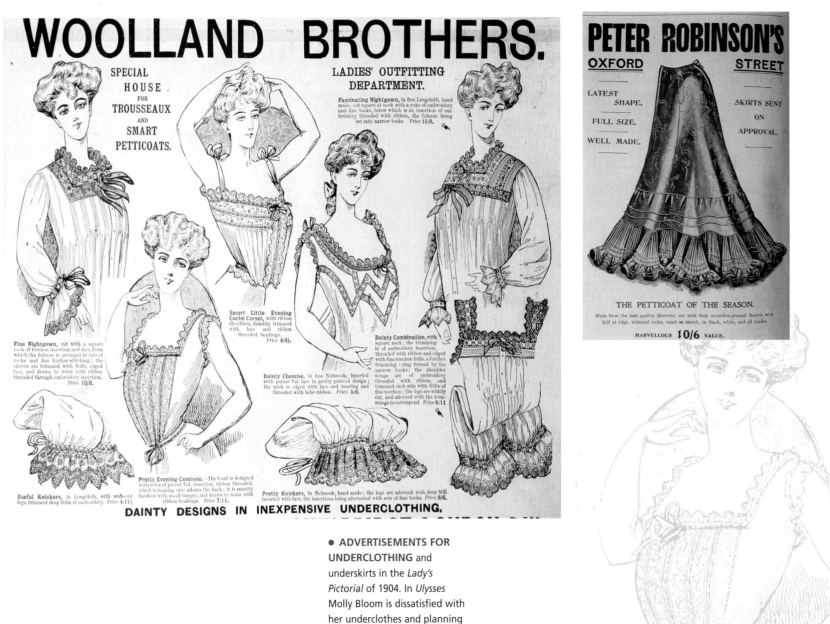

WOOLLAND BROTHERS.

SPECIAL HOUSE FOR TROUSSEAUX AND SMART PETTICOATS.

LADIES' OUTFITTING DEPARTMENT.

Fascinating Nightgown, in fine Longcloth, hand made, cut square at neck with a yoke of embroidery and fine tucks, below which is an insertion of embroidery threaded with ribbon, the fulness being set into narrow tucks. Price 15/9.

Smart Little Evening Cache Corset, with ribbon shoulders, daintily trimmed with lace and ribbon threaded beadings. Price 4/6½.

Fine Nightgown, cut with a square neck of torchon insertion and lace, from which the fulness is arranged in sets of tucks and fine feather-stitching; the sleeves are trimmed with frills, edged lace, and drawn to wrist with ribbon threaded through embroidery insertion. Price 10/9.

Dainty Chemise, in fine Nainsook, inserted with patent Val. lace in pretty pointed design; the neck is edged with lace and beading and threaded with bébé ribbon. Price 5/6.

Dainty Combination, with square neck; the trimming is of embroidery insertion, threaded with ribbon and edged with fine torchon frills, a further trimming being formed by the narrow tucks; the shoulder straps are of embroidery threaded with ribbon, and trimmed each side with frills of fine torchon; the legs are widely cut, and adorned with the trimmings to correspond. Price 6/11.

Pretty Evening Camisole.—The front is designed with rows of patent Val. insertion, ribbon threaded, which trimming also adorns the back; it is smartly finished with small basque, and drawn to waist with ribbon beadings. Price 7/11.

Useful Knickers, in Longcloth, with wide-cut legs, trimmed deep frills of embroidery. Price 4/11½.

Pretty Knickers, in Nainsook, hand made; the legs are adorned with deep frill inserted with lace, the insertions being alternated with sets of fine tucks. Price 9/6.

DAINTY DESIGNS IN INEXPENSIVE UNDERCLOTHING.

PETER ROBINSON'S
OXFORD   STREET

LATEST SHAPE.

FULL SIZE.

WELL MADE.

SKIRTS SENT ON APPROVAL.

THE PETTICOAT OF THE SEASON.

Made from the best quality Moirette, cut with deep accordion-pleated flounce with frill at edge, trimmed tucks, exact as sketch, in black, white, and all shades.

MARVELLOUS **10/6** VALUE.

● **ADVERTISEMENTS FOR UNDERCLOTHING** and underskirts in the *Lady's Pictorial* of 1904. In *Ulysses* Molly Bloom is dissatisfied with her underclothes and planning to buy new garments.

EARLY BIOGRAPHY

● **THE JOYCE FAMILY, SEPTEMBER 1888,** showing James aged six, his mother May, his father John Stanislaus and his maternal grandfather James Murray.

Courtesy of the Poetry/Rare Books Collection, University Libraries, State University of New York at Buffalo

● **HIGHER LINE LIBRARY, CLONGOWES WOOD COLLEGE, CO. KILDARE.** James Joyce attended this boarding school between 1888 and 1891.

● **JOYCE AS A CHILD.** James Joyce aged six-and-a-half.

Courtesy of the Poetry/Rare Books Collection, University Libraries, State University of New York at Buffalo

● **BELVEDERE COLLEGE PROGRAMME COVER.** Programme for the 'Gymnastic and Theatrical Entertainment' in Belvedere College, January 1898. Joyce, aged fifteen, took part in a production of F. Anstey's *Vice versa* as Dr Grimstone.

MUSIC.

Band of 1st Durham Light Infantry,

By permission of Officer commanding and Officers.

Overture	"Couronne d'Or,"	Herman.
Valse	"Sobre las Olas,"	Rosas.
Valse	"Donauwellen,"	Ivanovici.
Valse	"L'Etoile Polaire,"	Waldteufel.
Galop	"Postillion,"	Allen.
Valse	"Children's Carnival,"	Giehrer.
Valse	"Incognita,"	Ivanovici.
March	"Washington Post,"	Sousa.
March	"Castaldo,"	Novacek.
Serenade	"The Warblers,"	Perry.

MR. A. HIND, Band Master.

WINNERS OF IRISH SHIELD, 1896-1897.
S. Tanner, W. Carroll, C. Burgess, H. Kenny, R. Bonham,
J. Lemass, J. Molloy, F. Scott.

Drill and Gymnastic Instructor to College,

SERGEANT-MAJOR WRIGHT,

Army Gymnastic Staff.

A. M. D. G.

Belvedere College, S.J.

GYMNASTIC

AND

Theatrical

Entertainment,

MONDAY & TUESDAY,

JANUARY 10th & 11th, 1898.

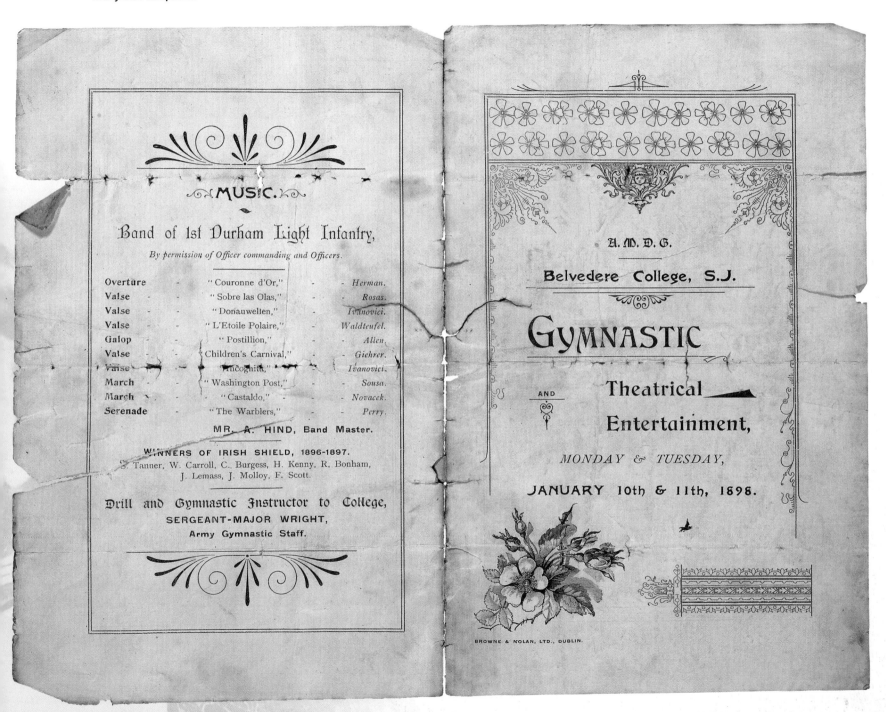

BROWNE & NOLAN, LTD., DUBLIN.

● **BELVEDERE COLLEGE,**
Great Denmark Street, which
James Joyce attended from
1893 to 1898.

Derek Stanley, *Central Dublin* (Gill and
Macmillan, 1999)

● **BRAY,** Co. Wicklow, where
the Joyce family lived between
1887 and 1891.

● 'CUPID'S CONFIDANTE'.
Programme for Miss Margaret
Sheehy's Dramatic and Musical
Recital, Tuesday, 8 January
1901. Joyce, who was friendly
with the Sheehy family, took
part in the sketch 'Cupid's
confidante' as 'Geoffrey
Fortescue, an Adventurer'.

● **JOYCE WITH STUDENTS.**
James Joyce with fellow students from University College. Joyce is second from left in the back row. Also pictured are George Clancy (Davin in *A portrait of the artist as a young man*), wearing a mortar board, and Joyce's close friend Con Curran (seated, far right), who is referred to in *Ulysses* as one of Stephen Dedalus's creditors.

● **BA DEGREE RESULTS,**
Royal University of Ireland examinations, 1902. Joyce's name and that of his friend Constantine Curran appear in the pass list.

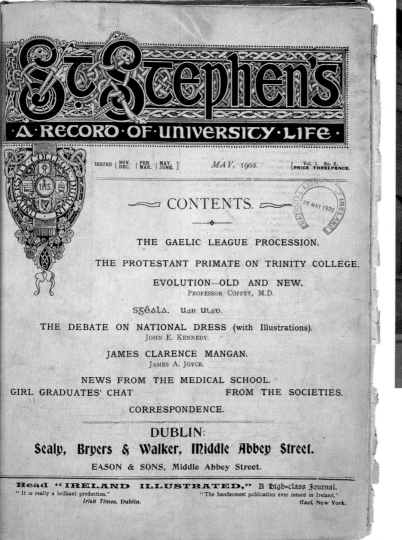

CATHOLIC UNIVERSITY. DUBLIN. 8598. W.L.

● **NEWMAN HOUSE,**
University College, St Stephen's
Green, which Joyce attended
between 1898 and 1902.

● *ST STEPHEN'S* **MAGAZINE, MAY 1902.** *St Stephen's* was the
student magazine of University College, and this edition carried the
text of a paper on the poet James Clarence Mangan given by James
Joyce to the college Literary and Historical Society in February.

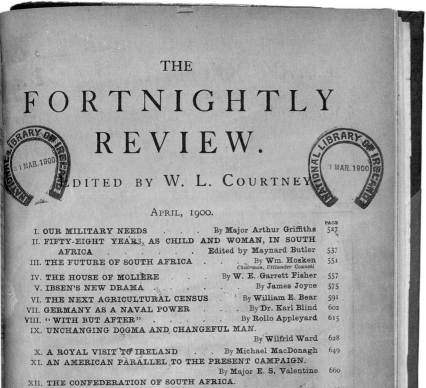

● *THE FORTNIGHTLY REVIEW,* APRIL 1900, which carried an article by the eighteen-year-old James Joyce on 'Ibsen's new drama'. It was his first published work.

● *THE VENTURE: AN ANNUAL OF ART AND LITERATURE,* 1904, in which 'Two songs' by James Joyce appeared. In 1904 he had also had several short stories published in the periodical *The Irish Homestead,* but this was his first publication in book form.

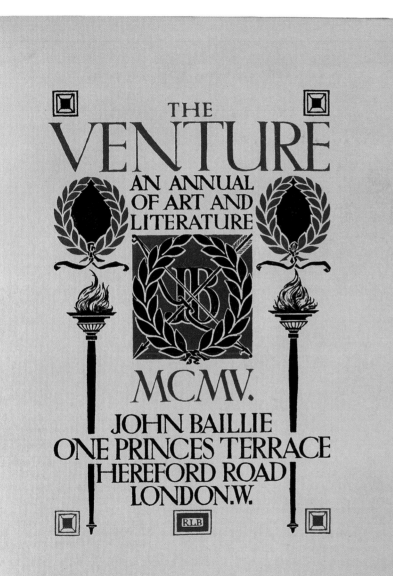

THE
VENTURE
AN ANNUAL
OF ART AND
LITERATURE

MCMV.

JOHN BAILLIE
ONE PRINCES TERRACE
HEREFORD ROAD
LONDON.W.

R.I.B

● *THE VENTURE* title page.

● **JAMES JOYCE IN PARIS, 1902,** where he lived between December 1902 and April 1903 until his mother's illness brought him back to Dublin.

Courtesy of the Beinecke Rare Book and Manuscript Library, Yale University

● **MARTELLO TOWER,** Sandycove, Co. Dublin. Joyce spent some time living with Oliver St John Gogarty in the tower in 1904.

• JAMES JOYCE, 1904, in a photograph taken by his friend Constantine Curran.

• CONCERT ADVERTISEMENT, AUGUST 1904. James Joyce is listed among the 'prominent artistes' who were to perform. He had a pleasant tenor voice and toyed with the idea of pursuing a professional career.

EXHIBITION
— OF —
Irish Industries,
ANTIENT CONCERT ROOM
BUILDINGS,
Horse Show Week,
Aug. 22 to 27.
ENTRANCE SIXPENCE.

Grand Gaelic Concerts

"Kindly Irish of the Irish;
Neither Saxon nor Italian."

WILL BE HELD ON

Thursday, Friday, Saturday,
AT 8 O'CLOCK.

SEVERAL PROMINENT ARTISTES WILL
CONTRIBUTE INCLUDING :

J. C. Doyle, J. F. McCormack, Cathal
McGarvey, Mr. J. C. Browner, Mr.
James A. Joyce, Mr. J. Hallissey, Miss
Agnes Treacy, Miss Olive Barry,
Keating Dancers, Etc., Etc.

ADMISSION   -   2s., 1s. & 6d.

LITERARY REVIVAL

LADY
GREGORY.

● **LADY AUGUSTA GREGORY (1852–1932)** by 'Bay' of Dublin. She was a playwright, a populariser of Irish mythology and a founder member of the Abbey Theatre, who showed Joyce considerable kindness, helping him to obtain a job writing reviews for the Dublin *Daily Express* and providing him with funds when he left Dublin with Nora.

● **ABBEY THEATRE OPENING PERFORMANCES.** Poster advertising the opening performances at the Abbey Theatre, Dublin, beginning on 27 December 1904. In the 'Scylla and Charybdis' episode of *Ulysses* Buck Mulligan anticipates this event.

JOHN MILLINGTON SYNGE.

● **JOHN MILLINGTON SYNGE (1871–1909),** Irish playwright and founder member of the Abbey Theatre, by 'Bay' of Dublin. He and Joyce met on several occasions in Paris in 1903.

● **IRISH NATIONAL THEATRE SOCIETY.** Sketch of rehearsals of an
Irish National Theatre Society production by George Russell, 'AE'
(1867–1935). The INTS was the forerunner of the Abbey Theatre and
had premises on Camden Street, where Joyce made a drunken scene
in 1904 (an incident referred to in *Ulysses*).

● **CAMDEN STREET.** Women
standing on Camden Street,
Dublin, where the INTS had its
premises.

● **WILLIAM BUTLER YEATS
(1865–1939),** poet, playwright
and founder member of the
Abbey Theatre, by 'Bay' of
Dublin.

W.B. YEATS.

● **BARTON MCGUCKIN (1852–1913)**, a famous Irish tenor who sang with the Carl Rosa Opera Company and who is reputed to have admired the voice of Joyce's father, John Stanislaus Joyce.

● **AMATEUR MUSICIANS.** *The Lady of the House*, Christmas 1901. The first page of this periodical emphasises the importance of music in Irish life at the period in which *Ulysses* is set.

● BUTLER'S MUSICAL
INSTRUMENTS, O'Connell
Bridge, which Leopold Bloom
passes in the 'Lestrygonians'
episode of *Ulysses*.

● **GRAND CONCERT PHONOGRAPH.** Advertisement for Edison's
Grand Concert Phonograph, 1903.

STUDIO: 11 HARCOURT STREET.

Ahead of all other Pianos

For **Quality** of **Tone**, **Touch**, **Superiority**
of **Workmanship**, **Finish**, and **Durability**, are

POHLMANN & Co.'s

Prize Medal PIANOS,

Whilst for CASH or EASY PAYMENTS they are cheapest of all.
Pianos, **Organs**, and **Harmoniums** by every maker
kept in stock and offered at prices or terms to suit all. Easy payments of 10s. 6d. per month. Catalogues free.

THE CECILIAN.

Are you Musical?

Then you'll appreciate the
marvellous performance of the
latest and greatest of all Piano-
Players, "The Cecilian." It
plays the world's music. Re-
citals daily. Inspection invited
by all interested in this Perfect
Player. Sole Agents, Pohlmann
and Co. See also our Grama-
phones, Columbiaphones, etc.

MUSIC.

Messrs. Pohlmann and Co. have now received
all this Season's New Music, which are
offered at lowest rates.

40 DAWSON ST., DUBLIN.

● **CECILIAN PIANO-PLAYER.**
Advertisement by Pohlmann
and Co. for the Cecilian
'Piano-Player', a self-playing
piano.

BUTLER'S Musical Instruments
OF EVERY DESCRIPTION.

Known all over the World and giving Universal Satisfaction.

Band Instruments.

BRASS, REED, FIFE & DRUM, OR ORCHESTRAL.

Rev. J. Verbrugge, Catholic Mission, Sandaken, B.N. Borneo, writes:—
I enclose cheque . . . during the 10 years I have been dealing with you . . . not one
Clarionet, Fife, &c., has cracked or gone out of tune, which is saying much in a Tropical and
damp climate like Borneo.

"Musicus," S.S. "Britton," Capetown, writes:—
The set of Clarionets I purchased give great satisfaction. They have travelled 80,000
miles, and have not been in the least affected by the climatic changes.

Band Instrument Catalogue B. (Illustrated), post free.

Graphophones.

Reproducing with absolute faithfulness any Musical Sound. A bevelled
Jewel running over smooth hard wax propelled by noiseless mechanism
ensures no sound but the sound of the Music being audible.
GRAND PRIX, PARIS, 1900.

The Popular, in Oak Case	£2 5 0
The Parlor (long winder)	£3 10 0
The Combination	£6 6 0

(All Record and Reproduce.)
Institutions not possessing a Band will find the "Grand" quite as
loud and clear as a Band of 8 performers.

Rev. Presidents, &c., should write for particulars of our "Special Facilities for Testing," and Special Lists.

Solo Instruments.

VIOLIN, in Case, with Bow, 20/-, 25/-, 30/-, & 40/-
Mandolines, Guitars, Banjoes, Auto-Harps,
Musical Boxes, with Interchangeable Tunes, from 12/6 to £50.
HARMONIUMS, with New "Voiced" Reeds.
AMERICAN ORGANS AND PIANOFORTES.

Catalogue A. (Illustrated) Post free.

MONUMENT HOUSE, **DUBLIN.**
O'CONNELL BRIDGE,
AND HAYMARKET, LONDON.

● **BUTLER'S MUSICAL
INSTRUMENTS.**
Advertisement for Butler's,
showing musical instruments
and 'graphophones', the
potential uses of which
intrigue Leopold Bloom.

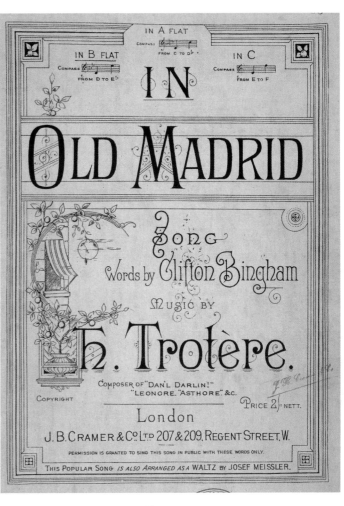

● *SINBAD THE SAILOR*. Programme for the Gaiety Theatre
pantomime *Sinbad the sailor*, 1892–3, referred to extensively in the
'Ithaca' episode of *Ulysses*.

● **'IN OLD MADRID'**. Sheet
music for the popular song 'In
old Madrid', a favourite of
Molly Bloom's.

● *SINBAD THE SAILOR.* Cast list for the Gaiety Theatre pantomime. Leopold Bloom sleepily thinks of the names Tinbad the Tailor and Whinbad the Whaler before he drifts off to sleep in the penultimate episode of *Ulysses*.

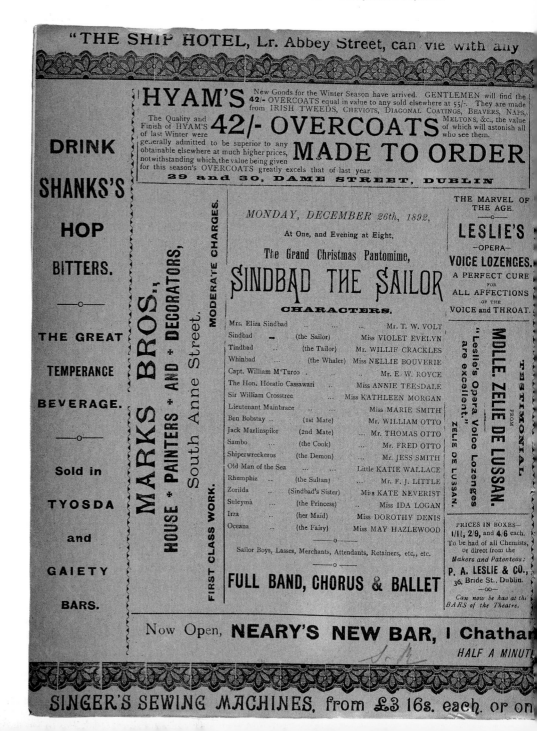

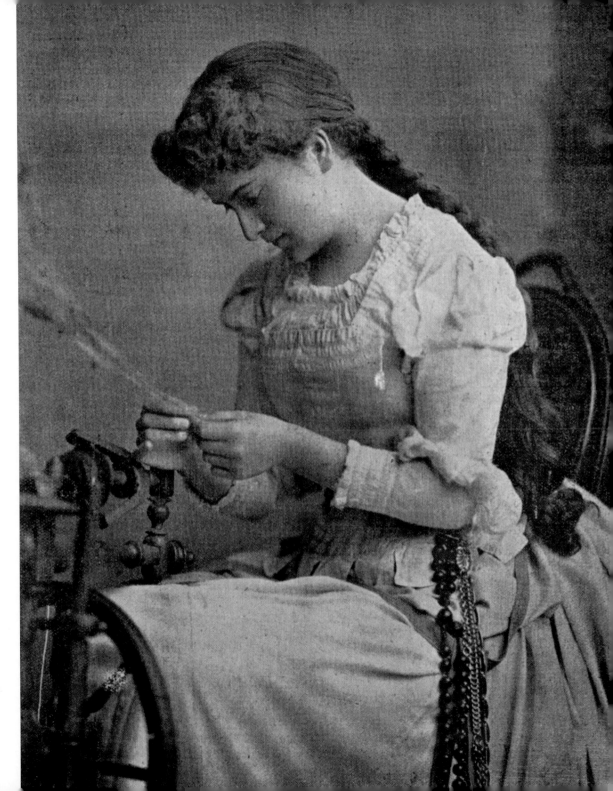

● **FANNY MOODY**
(1866–1945), soprano and
founder of the Moody-
Manners opera company with
her husband Charles Manners.
Touring opera companies such
as this one performed in
theatres in Dublin, presenting
several popular operas in a
week.

MR. CHARLES MANNERS, of the Moody-Manners Opera Company.

For Programme of the Week, see Page 9.

● CHARLES MANNERS (1857–1935), bass and founder of the Moody-Manners opera company with his wife Fanny Moody. Leopold Bloom considers setting up a rival opera company, with Molly as leading lady.

● THE CARL ROSA OPERA COMPANY. Flyer advertising the Carl Rosa Opera Company's visit to the Gaiety Theatre, 1900. Joyce attended performances of this touring opera company whenever possible, according to his friend J.F. Byrne.

● **MRS BANDMANN-PALMER.** Playbill for the Gaiety Theatre for the week beginning 13 June 1904. Millicent Palmer (1865–1905) was a well-known American actress whose roles included Hamlet. Leopold Bloom, who had seen her perform before, considers attending the performance of *Leah* on the evening of 16 June.

● **SIR HERBERT BEERBOHM TREE (1853–1917),** popular English actor-manager who performed periodically in Dublin.

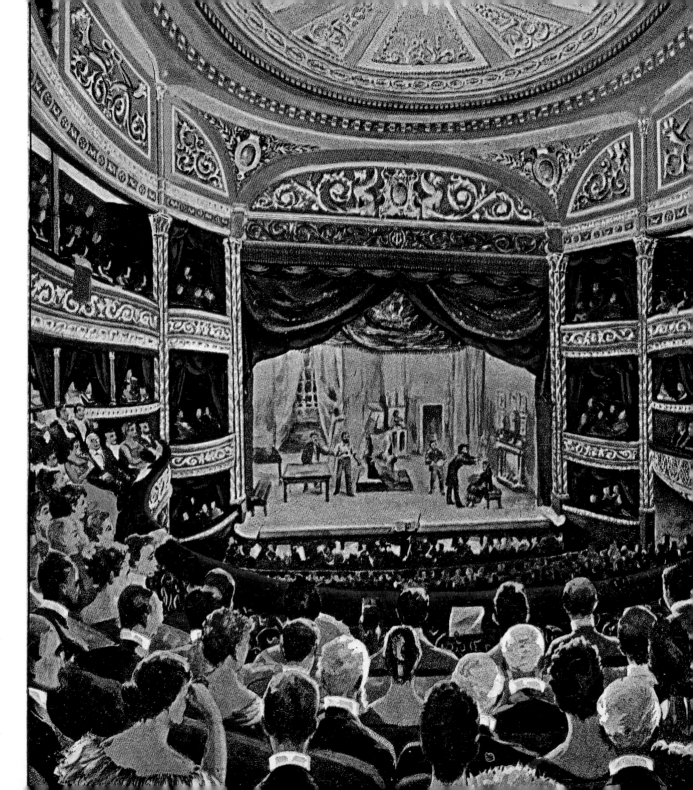

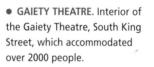 GAIETY THEATRE. Interior of the Gaiety Theatre, South King Street, which accommodated over 2000 people.

● 'POOLE'S MYRIORAMAS'.
Programme for 'Poole's
Myrioramas' with its 'Superb
Orchestral Bands', in the
Rotunda, Dublin, August 1902.
A Myriorama show was
typically made up of projected
images, cinematograph shorts
and vaudeville turns.

● **STAR VARIETIES.** Programme for the Star Theatre of Varieties, 1895. By 1904 the theatre had changed its name to the Empire Palace, but Dubliners still frequently referred to it as 'Dan Lowrey's', after the former managing director, seen on the programme here.

● **MOORE MEMORIAL CONCERT.** Programme for the Moore Memorial Concert, 1904. The songs of Thomas Moore (1779–1852) remained extremely popular in Ireland and elsewhere in 1904 and appear throughout Joyce's work.

● **STAR VARIETIES.** Programme for the Star Theatre of Varieties, 1892.

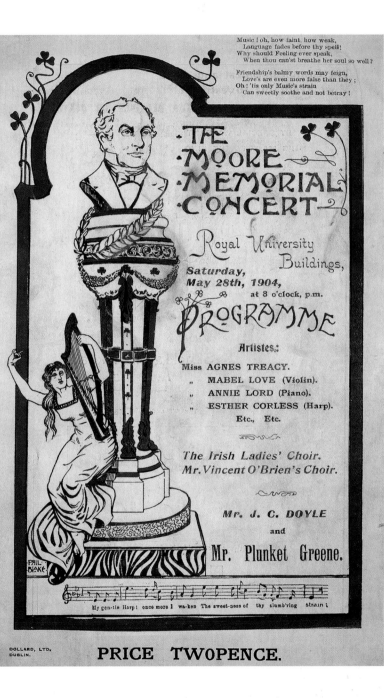

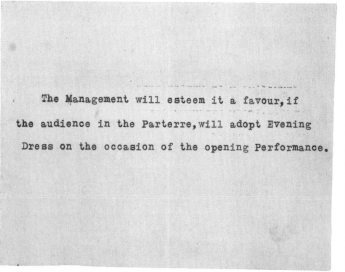

The Management will esteem it a favour, if the audience in the Parterre, will adopt Evening Dress on the occasion of the opening Performance.

● **DRESS CODE.** Notice from the management of the Theatre Royal, 1897.

● **THEATRE ROYAL,** Hawkins Street, 1904. This building, which was demolished in 1934, frequently hosted visits from touring opera and theatrical companies.

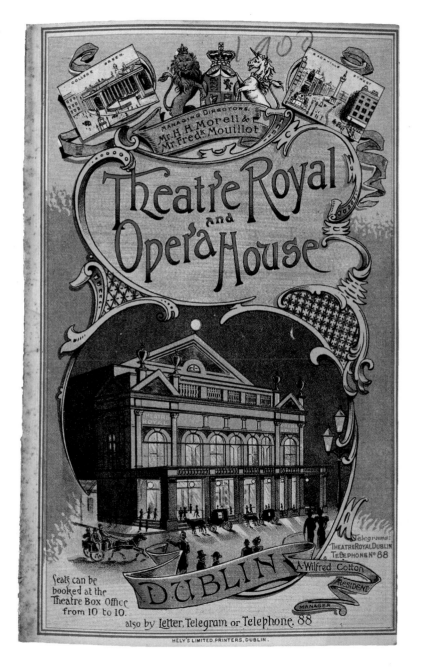

● **PROGRAMME** for the Theatre Royal, Hawkins Street, 1900.

● **THEATRE ROYAL** ticket stub, 1897.

● **EUGENE STRATTON.** Playbill for the Theatre Royal for the week beginning 13 June 1904. Eugene Stratton, who was appearing in the musical comedy *Fun on the Bristol,* was a well-known performer; posters advertising his appearance are mentioned in 'Hades' and 'Wandering Rocks' in *Ulysses.*

● **SIR JOHN MARTIN-HARVEY (1863–1944),** English actor and producer, who made a marked impression on Milly Bloom with his performance as Sydney Carton in *The only way.*

● **EMPIRE PALACE THEATRE.** Programme for the Empire Palace
Theatre, Dame Street, 1900. Comedienne Marie Kendall was the
main attraction on the evening of 16 June 1904.

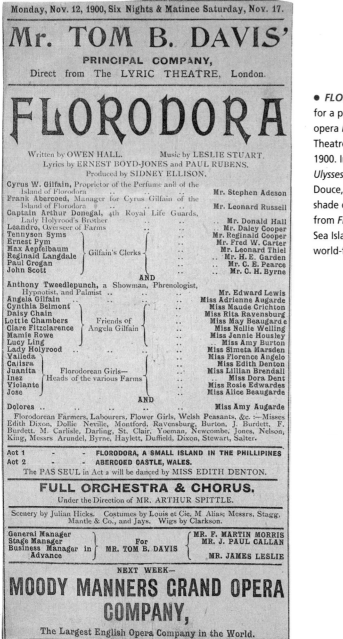

Monday, Nov. 12, 1900, Six Nights & Matinee Saturday, Nov. 17.

Mr. TOM B. DAVIS'
PRINCIPAL COMPANY,
Direct from The LYRIC THEATRE, London.

FLORODORA

Written by OWEN HALL.   Music by LESLIE STUART.
Lyrics by ERNEST BOYD-JONES and PAUL RUBENS.
Produced by SIDNEY ELLISON.

Cyrus W. Gilfain, Proprietor of the Perfume and of the Island of Florodora	Mr. Stephen Adeson
Frank Abercoed, Manager for Cyrus Gilfain of the Island of Florodora	Mr. Leonard Russell
Captain Arthur Donegal, 4th Royal Life Guards, Lady Holyrood's Brother	Mr. Donald Hall
Leandro, Overseer of Farms	Mr. Daley Cooper
Tennyson Syms	Mr. Reginald Cooper
Ernest Pym	Mr. Fred W. Carter
Max Aepfelbaum	Mr. Leonard Thiel
Reginald Langdale — Gilfain's Clerks	Mr. H. E. Garden
Paul Crogan	Mr. C. E. Pearce
John Scott	Mr. C. H. Byrne

AND

Anthony Tweedlepunch, a Showman, Phrenologist, Hypnotist, and Palmist	Mr. Edward Lewis
Angela Gilfain	Miss Adrienne Augarde
Cynthia Belmont	Miss Maude Crichton
Daisy Chain	Miss Rita Ravensburg
Lottie Chambers — Friends of	Miss May Beaugarde
Clare Fitzclarence — Angela Gilfain	Miss Nellie Welling
Mamie Rowe	Miss Jennie Housley
Lucy Ling	Miss Amy Burton
Lady Holyrood	Miss Simeta Marsden
Valleda	Miss Florence Angelo
Calisra	Miss Edith Denton
Juanita — Florodorean Girls—	Miss Lillian Brendall
Inez — Heads of the various Farms	Miss Dora Dent
Violante	Miss Rosie Edwardes
Jose	Miss Alice Beaugarde

AND

Dolores	Miss Amy Augarde

Florodorean Farmers, Labourers, Flower Girls, Welsh Peasants, &c.:—Misses Edith Dixon, Dollie Neville, Montford, Ravensburg, Burton, J. Burdett, F. Burdett, M. Carlisle, Darling, St. Clair, Yoeman, Newcombe, Jones, Nelson, King, Messrs Arundel, Byrne, Haylett, Duffield, Dixon, Stewart, Salter.

Act 1	-	FLORODORA, A SMALL ISLAND IN THE PHILLIPINES
Act 2	-	ABERCOED CASTLE, WALES.

The PAS SEUL in Act 2 will be danced by MISS EDITH DENTON.

FULL ORCHESTRA & CHORUS,
Under the Direction of MR. ARTHUR SPITTLE.

Scenery by Julian Hicks.   Costumes by Louis et Cie, M Alias; Messrs, Stagg, Mantle & Co., and Jays.   Wigs by Clarkson.

General Manager		MR. F. MARTIN MORRIS
Stage Manager	For	MR. J. PAUL CALLAN
Business Manager in Advance	MR. TOM B. DAVIS	MR. JAMES LESLIE

NEXT WEEK—

MOODY MANNERS GRAND OPERA COMPANY,

The Largest English Opera Company in the World.

● *FLORODORA*. Programme for a performance of the light opera *Florodora* in the Theatre Royal, November 1900. In the 'Sirens' episode of *Ulysses* the barmaid, Miss Douce, sings a line from 'The shade of the palm', a song from *Florodora*, set on a South Sea Island that produces a world-famous perfume.

MR JOSEPH MAAS

● JOSEPH MAAS (1847–86), a famous English tenor who performed with the Carl Rosa Opera Company.

● **JENNY LIND**, the 'Swedish Nightingale' (1820–87), one of the most popular musical performers of the nineteenth century. Leopold Bloom, in the 'Sirens' episode, recalls that a soup was named after her.

DRAWN ON STONE BY D. FABRONIUS, FROM A DAGUERREOTYPE, BY EDWARD KILBURN, ESQ.

● **ENRICO CARUSO (1873–1921)**, world-famous Italian tenor and one of the first major artists to make numerous recordings.

● **MINNIE HAUCK (1852–1929)**, an American soprano who sang the role of Carmen in the Gaiety Theatre. The talking fan carried by whore-mistress Bella Cohen in the 'Circe' episode is described as resembling that of Minnie Hauck in *Carmen*.

● **SMOKING CONCERTS.**
Review of recent 'Smoking
Concerts' in the *Irish Playgoer*,
1900.

SMOKING CONCERTS.

CATHOLIC COMMERCIAL CLUB.

The third concert of the session, held at the
club on Monday last, was a marked success, both
as regards the attendance and the programme.
The artistes were Miss Brady, Mrs. J Telford, Mr.
Evan Cox, Mr. J. F. Farrelly and A. Gaynor
(humorous), each of whom gave the items allotted
to them so effectively that encores became quite
the rule. Messrs. Boland and Cahill, a pair of
clever mandolinists, appeared in the character of
musical grotesques, and both pleased and amused
the audience, and in the second part these gentlemen and two others assumed the character of
musical pierrots, and gave a really excellent performance. It is their intention to form a large
troupe under this title, and their performance on
Monday gives promise that the idea should be a
success.

● **KINGSTOWN PAVILION.**
Detail from a programme of
orchestral performances,
Kingstown Pavilion and
Gardens, June 1903.

● **JOHN McCORMACK**
(1884–1945), internationally
renowned tenor and one of
Ireland's best-loved performers,
by Grace Gifford. In *Ulysses* it is
suggested that he is to perform
on the concert tour in which the
soprano Molly Bloom is to take
part.

● **FEIS CEOIL, 1903.** Programme for the Feis Ceoil, the Irish National Music Festival, May 1903. The tenor John McCormack took first place in that year, with very little formal training.

● **FEIS CEOIL, 1904.** Programme for the Feis Ceoil, the Irish National Music Festival, May 1904. James Joyce, a tenor, was awarded the bronze medal; he was prevented from attaining a higher placement by his inability to read music on sight.

● **PROGRAMME** for the Tivoli Theatre of Varieties, Burgh Quay.

● **'TURNS'**. Programme of 'turns' at the Tivoli Theatre of Varieties for the week beginning 13 June 1904.

PROGRAMME.

WEEK COMMENCING

MONDAY, JUNE 13th, 1904,

And during the Week.

| General Manager | ... | Mr. CHARLES M. JONES, |
| Secretary | ... | Mr. H. A. MURPHY |

1 Overture	- "Pigmy Dance." -	(Stretton)
2 Lily FOY -	- - -	Comedienne
3 3 DONALS -	-	The Gladiators on the Silver Chains
4 Len LEVER	- -	Coon Vocalist
5 Fred HARCOURT	The Modern Magician	
6 Interval Selection— "The Recruit " (Rensch)		
7 Lilian WARREN -	-	Vocal Picturee
8 The Mysterious LILITH -	-	The Sensation of Modern Times
9 The SALETOS -	Continental Gymnasts	
10 W. J. CHURCHILL	-	Comedian
11 ELLIE & EDGAR	Tight Wire Experts	
12 RITA & ROMA -	-	Speciality Artistes
Tivoli Orchestra -	E. J. TAYLOR, Conductor.	

The Public can leave the Theatre at the end of the Performance by all Exit and Entrance Doors, which must open outwards.

The Fire Resisting Screen in the Proscenium Opening will be lowered at least once during every Performance to ensure its being in perfect working order.

All Gangways, Passages, and Staircases must be kept free from chairs or any other obstruction, whether permanent or temporary.

PROGRAMME.

MONDAY, JUNE 13th, 1904,

AND EACH EVENING DURING THE WEEK.

1—Overture - "Stradella," - *Flotow*

2—The Cecils, Duettists and Dancers

3—Steve McCarthy, Eccentric Comedian

4—Jessie Albini, The Clever Comedienne

5—Frank Sylvo, The Quaint Comedy Juggler

6—Ray Wallace, The Premier Lady Mimic

7—Selection - "Carmen," - *Bizet*

8—Lennard & White, Coon Entertainers, &c.

9—Marie Kendal, The Favourite Comedienne

10—Sisters Dacre, Duettists and Dancers

11—The Leggetts, Comedy Sketch Artistes

12—Empire Animated Pictures

March—"Stars and Stripes for Ever," - *Sousa*

13—HYNES' RESTAURANT. Dinners, Suppers, Oysters, &c. WINES, SPIRITS, AND OTHER LIQUORS AT POPULAR PRICES.

☛ Owing to the extreme length of the Programme, the Public are respectfully requested not to indulge in indiscriminate ENCORES, otherwise part of it must necessarily be omitted.

● **PROGRAMME FOR THE EMPIRE PALACE THEATRE,** for the week beginning 13 June 1904 (*Ulysses* is set on 16 June 1904).

● **'THE MAN THAT BROKE THE BANK AT MONTE CARLO'.** Sheet music for a popular song that Joyce himself is reputed to have enjoyed performing.

Dublin. National Library.

P. 5041

● **THE NATIONAL LIBRARY OF IRELAND,** seen from the National
Museum, Kildare Street.

● **THOMAS WILLIAM LYSTER (1855–1922),** librarian of the National Library, in his office in 1897. He appears under his own name in the episode of *Ulysses* set in the National Library, 'Scylla and Charybdis'.

● **NATIONAL LIBRARY INTERIOR** *c.*1900, showing readers in the Reading Room.

NATIONAL LIBRARY of IRELAND.
KILDARE S? DUBLIN.

● **A NATIONAL LIBRARY POSTCARD.**

● **TWO GENTLEMEN IN THE PORCH** of the National Library, photographed by J.J. Clarke between 1897 and 1904. Many readers, including Joyce and his friends, would gather in the library porch to chat, debate, flirt and smoke.

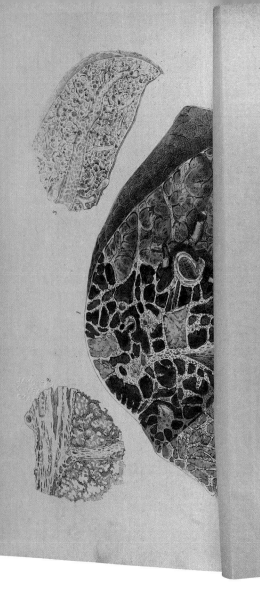

A TREATISE

ON THE

DISEASES OF THE OX;

BEING A

MANUAL OF BOVINE PATHOLOGY

ESPECIALLY ADAPTED FOR THE USE OF VETERINARY
PRACTITIONERS AND STUDENTS.

BY

JOHN HENRY STEEL, F.R.C.V.S., F.Z.S., A.V.D.,

LATE FELLOW OF THE UNIVERSITY OF BOMBAY
AND PROFESSOR OF VETERINARY SCIENCE AND PRINCIPAL
BOMBAY VETERINARY COLLEGE;
FORMERLY DEMONSTRATOR OF AND LECTURER ON ANATOMY AT THE
ROYAL VETERINARY COLLEGE OF LONDON.

FIFTH EDITION.

LONDON:
LONGMANS, GREEN, AND CO.,
AND NEW YORK: 15 EAST 16th STREET.
1895.

6192

● *DISEASES OF THE OX*, 1895. Joyce exploded with laughter when
he found a friend consulting this work in the National Library's
Reading Room, causing them both to be ejected by the librarian, an
incident that appears in *A portrait of the artist as a young man*.

● **LIBRARY ATTENDANT AND BOY ATTENDANT** behind the counter of the Reading Room in the National Library, photographed by J.J. Clarke between 1897 and 1904.

● **FR DINNEEN SILHOUETTE.** A silhouette of Father Dinneen, noted lexicographer and scholar, from the Library's staff scrapbooks. Fr Dinneen (1860–1934) appears as one of the National Library's readers in *Ulysse*s.

● **HAMLET.** Actor playing the role of Hamlet; Stephen Dedalus airs his theory of Shakespeare's *Hamlet* in the episode of *Ulysses* set in the Library.

POLITICS

● 'WHAT VILLAINS HAVE
DONE THIS?', supplement to
the *Weekly Freeman* of 13
May 1882, showing the figure
of Erin repudiating the
Phoenix Park Murders. On 6
May a group of extreme
nationalists calling themselves
the 'Invincibles' assassinated
the chief secretary and the
under-secretary for Ireland,
Lord Frederick Cavendish and
T.H. Burke, as they were
walking in the Phoenix Park.
This incident is referred to
several times in *Ulysses*.

PORTION OF A PROCLAMATION

By the Lord Lieutenant-General and General Governor of Ireland, dated 10th day of November, 1882.

SPENCER.

WE ARE PLEASED TO OFFER

A REWARD

OF

ONE THOUSAND

POUNDS

AND A

FREE PARDON

To any Person concerned in or privy to the

MURDERS OF THE CHIEF & UNDER SECRETARIES,

ON 6th MAY LAST,

(Not being one of the four actual perpetrators who drove away from the scene on a Car), who shall, within Three Months from the date hereof, give such *Private Information* as shall lead to the conviction of any one of the said four Murderers, or of any other person concerned in or privy to the Murders.

● **PHOENIX PARK MURDERS REWARD.** Proclamation of the reward offered for information on the Phoenix Park Murders, 10 November 1882.

ANOTHER TRIUMPH FOR JONATHAN.—BIGGEST REPTILE IN THE UNIVERSE.

● **POLITICAL CARTOON IN** *JUDY*, **17 MAY 1882,** depicting the Irish political violence as linked to extreme Irish nationalism in America.

● **'THE UNITED AMERICAN NATION'**, by Tom Merry, *St Stephen's Review*, 11 April 1891, showing an array of racial stereotypes, including an Irish agitator.

● **'THIS DEVIL'S WORK'**, supplement to the *Weekly Freeman*, 3 March 1888, casting Arthur Balfour, chief secretary for Ireland, in a devilish light.

LOOK AT "LOYAL" ULSTER!!!

THE ORANGE NAY! (? NEIGH.)
The "Ditch-liners" of the North give a decisive and characteristic answer to the Home Rule Question.

● **'LOOK AT "LOYAL" ULSTER'**, supplement to the nationalist *Weekly Freeman*, 19 June 1886, depicting brutish-looking loyalist rioters in Ulster. Urban unrest in Ulster had followed the defeat of the first Home Rule Bill earlier in June. In *Ulysses* Leopold Bloom's desk contains a sealed prophecy regarding the consequences of that bill, never unsealed because the bill never became law.

● **'THE ORANGE NAY! (NEIGH)'**, supplement to the *Weekly Freeman*, 15 May 1886, caricaturing the loyalist response to the prospect of Home Rule for Ireland.

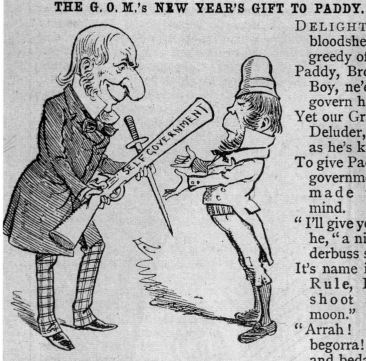

THE G. O. M.'s NEW YEAR'S GIFT TO PADDY.

DELIGHTING in bloodshed, and greedy of pelf, Paddy, Broth of a Boy, ne'er could govern himself; Yet our Grand Old Deluder, as wise as he's kind, To give Paddy self-government has made up his mind. "I'll give you," says he, "a nice blunderbuss soon, It's name is Home Rule, Pat, to shoot at the moon." "Arrah! musha! begorra! ochone! and bedad!"

Says Pat, "to possess that same goon I'll be glad.
I'll shoot at the moon, now and then, for a spree,
But to pick down a landlord's more plisant to me.
'Tis myself will be soon afther doing that same;
Shure I'll bag thim by hundreds—it's iligant game.
So my blessings, you Grandest and Ouldest of Min,
Will attend you for iver and all of your kin.
Whin an iligant goon and a beautiful pike
Will enable mesilf to destroy whom I like—
Or rather dislike; thin farewell to all sorrow,
Arrah! musha! ochone! and bedad! and begorra!"

● **'WEDDED!'**, by Tom Merry, *St Stephen's Review*, 27 June 1891, depicting Home Rule as a withered corpse.

● **ANTI-HOME-RULE VERSES** from the magazine *Judy*, 1886, caricaturing Irish aspirations to self-government.

LEAFLET No. 80.]   [SEVENTH SERIES.

Shall Ireland
have
Home Rule?

GLADSTONIAN REASONS EXAMINED.

[129

☞ This Leaflet is NOT copyright.

Disloyalty, Dishonesty, Conspiracy, Outrage,

AND THEN THE

HOME RULE BILL!

WHAT IS THOUGHT OF IT IN IRELAND?

The Capitalists are against it.
The Manufacturers are against it.
The Merchants are against it.
The Industrial Community are against it.
The Professional men are against it.
The Loyal men and women are against it.
All who have anything to lose are against it.

The Protestants of Ireland are against it—
    Episcopalians, over 600,000 ;
    Presbyterians and Methodists, over 500,000 ;
    Non-conformists of other Denominations, over 54,000.
        (See Census Returns of 1891.)

Don't imagine these are all in Ulster—
    Leinster has over 174,000 Protestants,
    Munster and Connaught over 106,000.
        (See Dublin Directory for 1893, page 637.)

The educated and loyal Roman Catholic laity of Ireland are
    against Home Rule.

WHO ARE IN FAVOUR OF HOME RULE?

The Dynamiters of America.
The Fenians and Invincibles of Ireland.
The illiterate voters of Ireland.
The idlers, the grumblers, and the disaffected.
The mutilators of cattle.
The boycotters, and other systematic law-breakers.
The moonlighters, and other perpetrators of outrage.
The place-hunters, who see no other prospect of earning money.

[P. T. O.

● **IRISH UNIONIST ALLIANCE LEAFLET,** 1893, showing the
British flag and outlining the case against granting Ireland Home
Rule.

● **IRISH UNIONIST ALLIANCE LEAFLET,** 1893,
characterising those who supported Home Rule as 'illiterate'
and 'dynamiters.'

● **'THE CROWBAR KING'** by Tom Merry, *St Stephen's Review*, 27 December 1890. This cartoon associates the Parliamentary politician Charles Stewart Parnell with violent forms of nationalist agitation. Two of the skulls adorning his throne bear the names 'Burke' and 'Cavendish', the two government officials assassinated in the Phoenix Park murders of 1882, which are referred to in *Ulysses*.

● **'THE FIGHT WITH APOLLYON'** by Tom Merry, *St Stephen's Review*, 15 December 1888. A bloodthirsty Parnell, transformed into the embodiment of evil from Bunyan's *Pilgrim's progress*, attacks the Union. On his wings the supporters of his allegedly violent campaign are identified, ranging from Gladstone to 'Dynamiters'.

SUPPLEMENT TO **THE NATION.** 21ST FEB., 1891.

THE UPLIFTING OF THE BANNER.
Erin to the Pretender.—"A VAY, WRECKER OF MY CAUSE!"

● **'THE UPLIFTING OF THE BANNER'**, *The Nation*, 21 February 1891. In this anti-Parnell cartoon, he is seen bringing 'shame, discord, ruin' on Erin as he tramples on morality and religion; this appeared in the aftermath of Parnell's involvement in the O'Shea divorce case and the bitter split in the Irish Parliamentary Party that followed. Joyce's father, John Stanislaus, remained a loyal supporter of Parnell throughout.

● **PORTRAIT OF CHARLES STEWART PARNELL** (1846–91) from the *Weekly Freeman*, 10 October 1891, following his death on 6 October.

● **'A XMAS GREETING TO WATERFORD',** *Weekly National Press*, 19 December 1891, caricaturing John Redmond as a devilish, divisive figure spreading hate and dissension. Redmond was a supporter of Parnell and took over the leadership of the Parnellite wing of the Irish Parliamentary Party after Parnell's death.

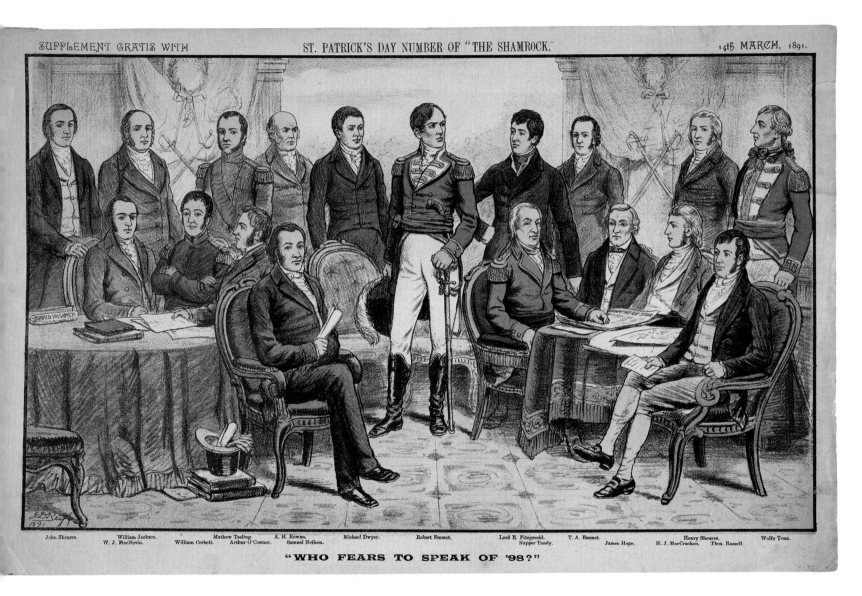

"WHO FEARS TO SPEAK OF '98?"

John Sheares.   William Jackson.   Mathew Teeling.   A. H. Rowan.   Michael Dwyer.   Robert Emmet.   Lord E. Fitzgerald.   T. A. Emmet.   Henry Sheares.   Wolfe Tone.
W. J. MacNevin.   William Corbett.   Arthur O'Connor.   Samuel Neilson.   Napper Tandy.   James Hope.   H. J. MacCracken.   Thos. Russell.

● **'WHO FEARS TO SPEAK OF '98?'**, *The Shamrock*, 14 March 1891, commemorating the ill-fated rebellion by the United Irishmen in 1798. Several of the figures illustrated here, including Emmet, Fitzgerald and Sheares, are mentioned in *Ulysses*.

ENLISTING IN THE ENGLISH ARMY IS TREASON TO IRELAND.

Go, to find 'mid crime and toil
   The doom to which such guilt is hurried!
Go, to leave on Afric's soil
   Your bones unbleached, accursed, unburied!
Go, to crush the just and brave,
   Whose wrongs with wrath the world are filling!
Go, to slay each brother-slave,
   Or spurn the blood-stained *Saxon Shilling!*

FELLOW-COUNTRYMEN—

The Irishmen in England's Service who are sent to South Africa will have to fight against Irish Nationalists who have raised Ireland's flag in the Transvaal, and have formed an Irish Brigade to fight for the Boers against the oppressor of Ireland.

Remember Ninety-Eight!
Remember the Penal Laws!
Remember the Famine!

England's Army is small. Englishmen are not good soldiers. England has to get others to do her fighting for her. In the past Irishmen have too often won battles for England, and saved her from defeat, and thus have riveted the chains upon their motherland! Let them do so no more.

Think of the ruined homes and of the Emigrant Ships. Within sixty years our population has been reduced by one-half as the direct result of English rule. The Boers are making a brave fight against this rule. Let no Irishman dare to raise a hand against them or for our enemy and their enemy—England!

In all our towns and villages we see the recruiting-sergeants trying to entrap thoughtless Irish boys into joining the British Army. The recruiting-sergeant is an enemy, and it is a disgrace to any decent Irishman to be seen in his company. But he should be watched and followed, and the boys whom he seeks to entrap should be warned and reasoned with.

In preventing recruiting for the English Army you are working for Ireland's honour, and you are doing something to help the Boers in their Struggle for Liberty.

By order,
IRISH TRANSVAAL COMMITTEE.
Dublin, 12th October, 1899.

"AND DON'T YOU FORGET IT."

4 MC

Dear Sir!
God save soon Ireland
And Transvaal too!
Hurrah for Liberty
In every Country!
If they fire you out
Dont' shut your mouth!
In danger you hear
God is the brave near!

Respectfully
Many American Boer Friends.

● **ANTI-BOER WAR POSTCARD** indicating American support for the Boers in South Africa and identifying Irish national aspirations with the Boer struggle against Great Britain.

● **ANTI-ENLISTMENT NOTICE,** 1899, urging Irishmen not to enlist in the British army fighting the Boer War (1899–1902) in South Africa; the Irish Transvaal Committee was a pro-Boer support group. In the final episode of *Ulysses,* Molly Bloom recalls a former lover who died in the Boer War.

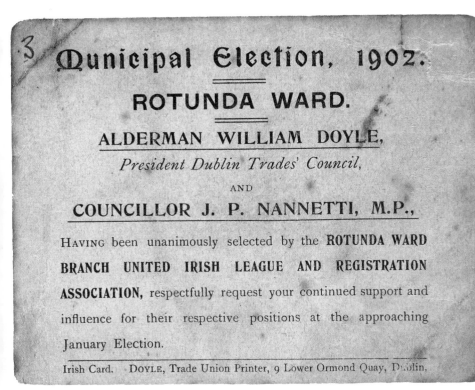

Municipal Election, 1902.

ROTUNDA WARD.

ALDERMAN WILLIAM DOYLE,

President Dublin Trades' Council,

AND

COUNCILLOR J. P. NANNETTI, M.P.,

HAVING been unanimously selected by the **ROTUNDA WARD**
BRANCH UNITED IRISH LEAGUE AND REGISTRATION
ASSOCIATION, respectfully request your continued support and
influence for their respective positions at the approaching
January Election.

Irish Card.   DOYLE, Trade Union Printer, 9 Lower Ormond Quay, Dublin,

● **ELECTION LITERATURE** for
Joseph P. Nannetti, 1902.
Nannetti was a Dublin MP in
1904 and appears in the
'Aeolus' episode in *Ulysses*.

● **'THE DOG TURNS ON HIS**
MASTER' from the *Weekly*
Freeman and National Press,
30 August 1902, depicting
Orangeism as a savage dog.
The artist, Phil Blake, is
mentioned in *Ulysses*.

SUPPLEMENT GIVEN AWAY WITH
THE WEEKLY FREEMAN AND NATIONAL PRESS, Saturday, August 30th, 1902.   Price Three-halfpence.

The Dog turns on his Master.
The Moral of the South Belfast Election.

HELY'S, LIMITED,   HIS MAJESTY'S ARRIVAL AT PUNCHESTOWN, APRIL, 1904.   DUBLIN.

16. 5. 04   From Ted.

● **EDWARD VII** at Punchestown
Races in April 1904; it was his
second visit to Ireland in two years
and provoked a broad spectrum of
response. The king's colourful past is
discussed irreverently in the
'Cyclops' episode of *Ulysses*.

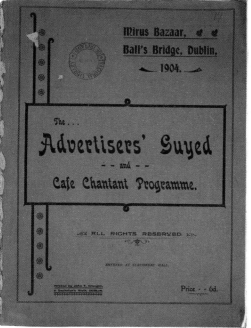

Mirus Bazaar,
Ball's Bridge, Dublin,
1904.

The...
Advertisers' Guyed
-- and --
Café Chantant Programme.

ALL RIGHTS RESERVED.

ENTERED AT STATIONERS' HALL.

Printed by John T. Drought,
6 Bachelor's Walk, DUBLIN.

Price - - 6d.

● **PROGRAMME** for the 'Café
Chantant' at the Mirus Bazaar,
May 1904. The Bazaar was
opened by the Irish lord
lieutenant and viceroy, the earl
of Dudley; this is mirrored in
Ulysses, although Joyce shifts
the date of the opening
ceremony from the end of May
to 16 June.

● **THE VICEREGAL LODGE,**
home of the Irish lord
lieutenant, in the Phoenix Park,
Dublin.

● **LADY DUDLEY,** wife of the
earl of Dudley, Irish viceroy
and lord lieutenant between
1902 and 1905, who is seen in
the viceregal cavalcade driving
through Dublin in *Ulysses*.

● **'THE BREAKDOWN'**, *Weekly Freeman and National Press*, 4 October 1902, caricaturing the British administration in Ireland. It shows the earl of Dudley, the Irish lord lieutenant, riding in a broken-down cart labelled 'Coercion'.

● **DUBLIN CASTLE**, the heart of the British administration in Ireland. Several of the characters in *Ulysses*, including Martin Cunningham, are employed as civil servants there.

● 'THE JEW QUESTION IN
IRELAND'. Following anti-
Semitic incidents in Limerick in
early 1904, the small Jewish
community in Ireland was the
focus of some public
discussion, as illustrated by this
article in the *Leader* of 4 June
1904.

THE LEADER.   JUNE 4, 1904.

these are mostly   **THE JEW QUESTION IN IRELAND.**

ous denominations, and are   AT the outset, I wish to make one thing as clear as
possible: I hold no brief for the Jews, nor

FURNITURE! FURNITURE!
Special Terms to Gaelic Leaguers.

JOHN S. KELLY, Limited,
(No connection with Jews),
Have opened complete House Furnishing Warerooms at
64 CAMDEN STREET, 64
Where Business will be carried on at Reduced Prices.
10 to 30 per cent. Cash or Terms
Less than any other House in the City.

IRISH MANUFACTURE A SPECIALITY.
We push Irish Goods where possible.

JOHN S. KELLY, Limited
(No connection with Jews),
64 CAMDEN ST.

● ANTI-SEMITIC
ADVERTISEMENT
Advertisement appearing in
the *Irish Rosary*, 1904; the firm
in question is at pains to note
that it has 'no connection with
Jews'.

RELIGION

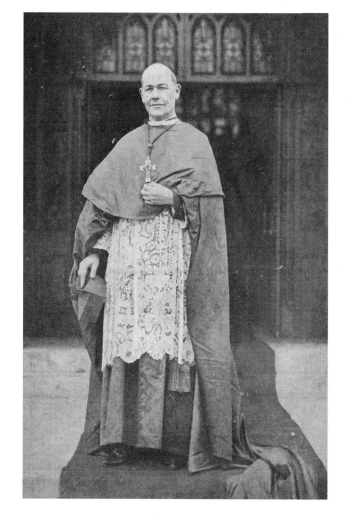

● 'HAND OFF, PRIEST!' by Tom Merry, *St Stephen's Review*, 25 July 1891, an unenthusiastic depiction of the significant role of the Catholic church in Irish life.

● CARDINAL VINCENT VANNUTELLI, who represented Pope Pius X at the dedication of the cathedral in Armagh in 1904. Joyce mischievously signed one of his letters in 1904 with this name.

● **GLASNEVIN CEMETERY** in Dublin, where a number of characters, including Leopold Bloom, attend a funeral in the 'Hades' episode of *Ulysses*. This illustration shows the O'Connell Monument, commemorating the nationalist leader Daniel O'Connell.

● **FATHER JOHN CONMEE** (1847–1910), a Jesuit priest who was on the staff of two of the schools Joyce attended, Clongowes Wood and Belvedere, and who plays a substantial role in the 'Wandering Rocks' episode of *Ulysses*.

● **ST ANDREW'S CATHOLIC CHURCH,** Westland Row, Dublin, referred to as 'All Hallows' church in *Ulysses*, after the monastery that earlier stood on the site. Leopold Bloom observes a service here with interest but without involvement.

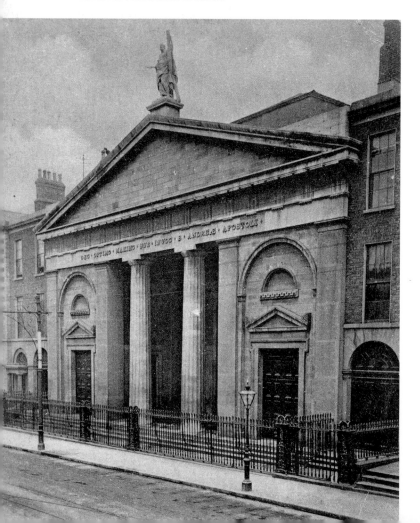

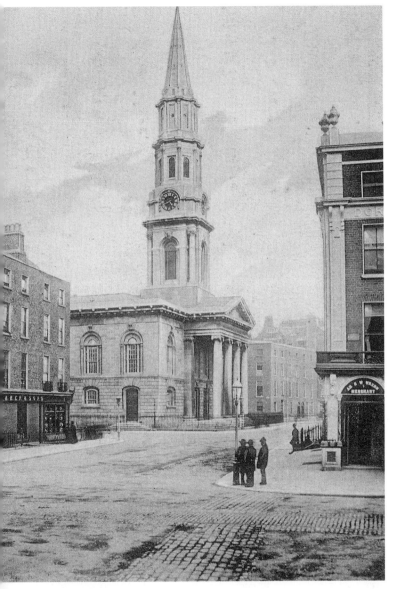

● **STAR OF THE SEA CHURCH,** Sandymount, where a temperance retreat takes place during the 'Nausicaa' episode of *Ulysses*.

● **ST GEORGE'S CHURCH OF IRELAND CHURCH,** Hardwicke Place, the bells of which are heard in No. 7 Eccles Street on the morning and evening of 16 June 1904.

Part 2 ABROAD

ABROAD

When James Joyce and Nora Barnacle left Ireland in October 1904, they made their way to the city of Trieste, now in Italy but then a part of the Austro-Hungarian empire. The expected job in a language school there did not materialise, and they went instead to Pola (now in Croatia), where Joyce began teaching English. By March of 1905 the family was living in Trieste. Apart from a brief period spent in Rome in 1906–7, they remained in Trieste (where they were joined by other members of the Joyce family) until forced to move to Zurich in 1915 by World War I. After 1920 the family lived mostly in France, especially Paris, where Joyce attracted the backing, financial and otherwise, of a number of patrons and supporters.

The selection of images in this part of the book focuses first on the personal and professional developments in Joyce's life after 1904 (apart from the two great works *Ulysses* and *Finnegans wake*). Photographs of the different cities in which the Joyce family lived are featured: Pola; Trieste, that linguistically and ethnically diverse and interesting city; Zurich, where Joyce met his great friend Frank Budgen; Paris, home to so many members of the Modernist community of writers in the 1920s. James and Nora's children, a son and a daughter, Giorgio and Lucia, born in 1905 and 1907, are depicted in some of the images chosen, while a selection of covers and other images illustrate the developments in Joyce's professional career. The important role played by friends and supporters in the development of that career is acknowledged in a section depicting a number of these figures.

Between the end of 1914 and its publication in February 1922, the writing of *Ulysses* consumed James Joyce to a greater and greater extent. The historical backdrop against which the novel was written is evoked from an Irish perspective, as a reminder that the first years of the composition of *Ulysses* took place in the shadow of World

War I and that, during the years in which Joyce was writing about the Dublin of 1904, contemporary Dublin witnessed the upheaval of insurrection, the Anglo-Irish War and civil strife. The novel's complex pre- and post-publication history is illustrated, from its first appearance in serial form to its publication by Shakespeare and Company in 1922 and the aftermath. A series of images evoke the extraordinary stages of its public reception—moral outrage, acclaim as a masterpiece, censorship, prohibition, piracy and eventual dissemination in a huge range of editions. Images of different editions of the novel are interwoven with postcards and photographs of the Dublin locations in which the episodes of the novel are set; as *Ulysses* in its various editions circulated widely, Dublin of 1904 would gain literary immortality.

Although the story of *Ulysses* only began with its publication in 1922, Joyce's attention was soon diverted to the work that would occupy most of the rest of his life, *Finnegans wake*. It appeared in a series of 'fragments' under the title 'Work in progress'; some of these are illustrated in the images focusing on Joyce's writing after *Ulysses*. The final photographs in the book bring us back once again to Ireland. They show the first Irish Bloomsday celebrations, when a group of Irish writers, including Patrick Kavanagh and Flann O'Brien, paid tribute to Joyce's great novel on the fiftieth anniversary of Bloomsday, 16 June 1954. They are fitting images with which to close this Joycean scrapbook, which celebrates one of the world's great writers.

TRIESTE AND POLA

● **COVER OF 'JAMES JOYCE: A LECTURE'**, delivered in Milan in 1927 by his friend Italo Svevo. It was translated from Italian by Stanislaus Joyce and published in 1950. Joyce became friendly with the writer Svevo (whose real name was Ettore Schmitz) in Trieste, where Svevo attended Joyce's English classes.

● **THE BERLITZ SCHOOL IN POLA** (modern-day Pula, in Croatia), where Joyce was employed as a teacher of English from late 1904 to early 1905.

Courtesy of the Trieste James Joyce Museum

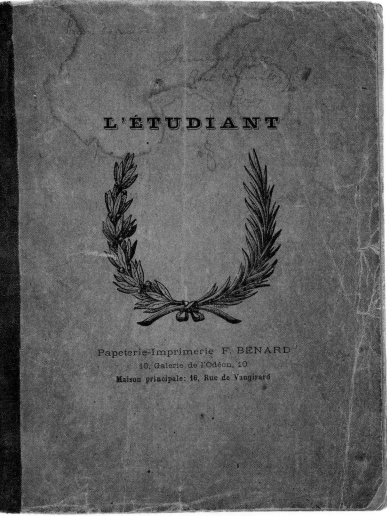

● **A VIEW OF THE CITY OF POLA,** where Nora and Joyce spent their first months together.

Courtesy of the Trieste James Joyce Museum

● **COVER OF THE 'PARIS–POLA COMMONPLACE BOOK',** an eclectic collection of Joyce's daily accounts, lists of authors and books he read or wanted to read, transcribed quotations, writings on aesthetics and notes for works he would write, as well as other curiosities. Joyce made notes in this book during his time in Paris in 1903 and after he left Ireland with Nora Barnacle in 1904.

Trieste.

● **TRIESTE** (then in Austria, now part of Italy), to where the Joyce family moved in March of 1905. Apart from some months in Rome in 1906–7, they remained in Trieste until forced by World War I to move to Zurich in Switzerland in 1915.

● **COVER OF** *STEPHEN HERO,* on which Joyce worked during his time in Pola and in Trieste. In 1907 he began to rewrite *Stephen Hero* as *A portrait of the artist as a young man,* and the earlier work was only published posthumously.

STEPHEN HERO

by

James Joyce

Pola.

Via Giulia

P. SCHÖLER, WIEN — 1381

● **VIA GIULIA, POLA.** Joyce
rented rooms at No. 2 on
arriving in Pola.

Courtesy of the Trieste James Joyce
Museum

● **ANOTHER VIEW OF
THE VIA GIULIA**

Courtesy of the Trieste James
Joyce Museum

LATER BIOGRAPHY AND WORKS

● **GIORGIO AND LUCIA JOYCE,** Joyce's two children, at the window of their Trieste apartment *c.* 1913.

Courtesy of the Poetry/Rare Books Collection, University Libraries, State University of New York at Buffalo

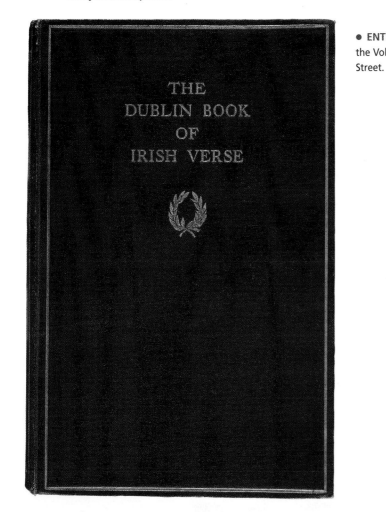

● ENTRANCE TICKET for the Volta Cinema, Mary Street.

● *THE DUBLIN BOOK OF IRISH VERSE*, **1909.** This contained three poems from Joyce's *Chamber music*, constituting their first publication in Ireland.

● **THE VOLTA CINEMA, MARY STREET, DUBLIN.** In partnership with Triestine businessmen, Joyce returned to Dublin in 1909 to open the city's first cinema, the Volta. The venture was not a success, and the cinema closed the following year.

● *DUBLINERS,* 1914. Joyce's short-story collection, on which he had been working since 1904, was eventually published by Grant Richards of London, after frustrating attempts to have it published in Dublin.

● **JOYCE WITH GUITAR.** James Joyce playing guitar, photographed by Ottocaro Weiss in Trieste, 1915.

Courtesy of the Poetry/Rare Books Collection, University Libraries, State University of New York at Buffalo

● **DETAIL FROM THE COVER OF** *GIACOMO JOYCE,* published posthumously in 1968, from a short manuscript in Joyce's hand written in Trieste.

● **ZURICH,** where the Joyce family lived for most of the period between 1915 and 1919.

Courtesy of the Baugeschichtliches Archiv der Stadt Zurich

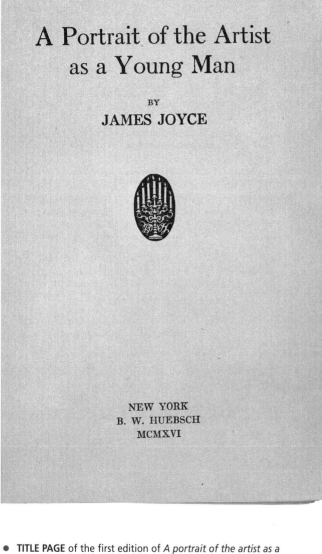

A Portrait of the Artist as a Young Man

BY

JAMES JOYCE

NEW YORK
B. W. HUEBSCH
MCMXVI

● **TITLE PAGE** of the first edition of *A portrait of the artist as a young man*, published in New York in 1916 by B.W. Huebsch. Huebsch became not only Joyce's American publisher but also a friend and supporter.

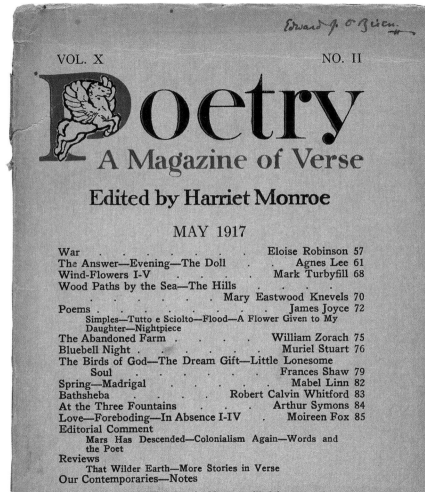

● **COVER OF *POETRY*,** an American magazine, May 1917, in which several of Joyce's poems appeared.

● **COVER OF *EXILES*,** 1918, Joyce's first and only play.

● **THE JOYCE FAMILY** lived
in Paris for much of the
period between 1920 and
1940. These images of the city
in the 1920s show a view of
the Eiffel Tower from the
Trocadéro Gardens, and the
quays with Notre Dame in the
background.

● **A VIEW OF THE PONT NEUF**, Paris.

● **THE JOYCES IN LONDON** on their wedding day, 4 July 1931, 27 years after they left Ireland together.

THE OBELISK PRESS
338 Rue Saint-Honoré, PARIS 1ᵉʳ

Please send me _a_ cop_y_ of "A Chaucer A.B.C
initials by Lucia Joyce, at 100 francs (enclosed)

Name

Address

● **ORDER FORM FOR** *A
CHAUCER ABC*, with initial
letters illuminated by Lucia
Joyce, published by Obelisk,
1936.

● **PICTURE POSTCARD** sent
by Joyce to Paul Léon in 1934
from Spa in Belgium.

illuminated

ebsch
BRO
WEDEN

● **LUCIA JOYCE (1907–1982),**
who illustrated certain
fragments of 'Work in progress'
with illuminated letters.

FRIENDS AND ASSOCIATES

● **FRANK BUDGEN (1882–1971)**, artist and author. Budgen was a close friend of Joyce in Zurich; he wrote and illustrated *James Joyce and the making of Ulysses* about this period in the author's life.

Courtesy of the University of Tulsa, Department of Special Collections

● **HARRIET SHAW WEAVER (1876–1961)**. Weaver was an important patron and supporter of Joyce throughout his life, both financially and otherwise. Appointed literary executor in Joyce's will, she fulfilled that final role with dedication.

Courtesy of the University of Tulsa, Department of Special Collections

● **JAMES JOYCE IN RELAXED POSE**, *c.* 1935, from the Léon Collection.

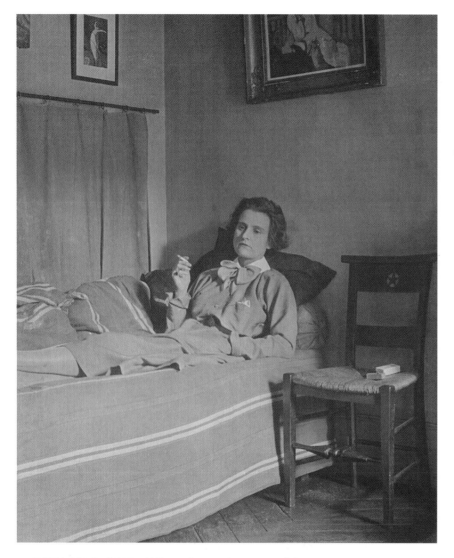

EX-LIBRIS

SHAKESPEARE AND COMPANY
SYLVIA BEACH
PARIS

● SHAKESPEARE AND
COMPANY BOOKPLATE.

● **SYLVIA BEACH (1887–1962)** was the American owner of the
Paris bookshop Shakespeare and Company, founded in 1919.
Shakespeare and Company published the first edition of *Ulysses* in
1922, and Beach was a loyal supporter and friend of Joyce for
many years.

LA MAISON DES AMIS DES LIVRES
7, rue de l'Odéon, Paris - VI° — Tél. : Fleurus 25-05

Mercredi 7 Décembre 1921
à 9 h. précises du soir

SÉANCE CONSACRÉE A
L'ÉCRIVAIN IRLANDAIS

JAMES JOYCE

CONFÉRENCE PAR

M. VALERY LARBAUD

Lecture de fragments de ULYSSES
traduits pour la 1ère fois en français

— Nous tenons à prévenir le public que certaines des pages qu'on lira sont
d'une hardiesse d'expression peu commune qui peut très légitimement choquer. —

Cette séance étant donnée au bénéfice de JAMES JOYCE,
le droit d'admission sera, exceptionnellement, de 20 francs par
personne. Nous serions particulièrement reconnaissants envers
les personnes qui voudraient bien dépasser la somme fixée.

Les places doivent être retenues à l'avance. Nous rappelons qu'elles sont limitées
à cent.

● **ANNOUNCEMENT OF VALERY LARBAUD'S PUBLIC LECTURE ON *ULYSSES*,** which took place in the bookshop La Maison des Amis des Livres.

● **JOYCE AND BEACH.** Joyce and Sylvia Beach outside Shakespeare and Company at 8 Rue Dupuytren, its first premises. In 1921 the shop moved to 12 Rue de l'Odéon.
Courtesy of the Poetry/Rare Books Collection, University Libraries, State University of New York at Buffalo

JAMES JOYCE

Advance Press Notices.

— Mr. EZRA POUND in — *Instigations* — His profoundest work... an impassioned meditation on life... He has done what Flaubert set out to do in Bouvard et Pécuchet, done it better, more succint.
— Mr. RICHARD ALDINGTON in — *The English Review* — A most remarkable book... Bloom is a rags and tatters Hamlet, a proletarian Lear... An astonishing psychological document... *ULYSSES* is more bitter, more sordid, more ferociously satirical than anything Mr. JOYCE has yet written... A tremendous libel on humanity which I, at least, am not clever enough to refute.
— THE OBSERVER — ...Whatever may be thought of the work, it is going to attract almost sensational attention.
— THE TIMES — ... ... of the utmost sincerity.... complete courage.
— Mrs. EVELYN SCOTT in — *The Dial* — A contemporary of the future... His technique has developed unique aspects that indicate a revolution of style for the future... This Irish artist is recreating a portion of the English language... He uses the stuff of the whole world to prove one man.
— THE NEW AGE — ..."One of the most interesting literary symptoms in the whole literary world, and its publication is very nearly a public obligation".
— Mr. VALERY LARBAUD in — *La Nouvelle Revue Française* — Avec *ULYSSES*, l'Irlande fait une rentrée sensationnelle et triomphante dans la haute littérature européenne.

ULYSSES suppressed four times during serial publication in " The Little Review" will be published by "SHAKESPEARE AND COMPANY" complete as written.

This edition is private and will be limited to 1.000 copies :

100 copies signed on Dutch hand made paper . . . . **350** fr.
150 copies on vergé d'Arches . . . . **250** fr.
750 copies on hand made paper . . . . **150** fr.

The work will be a volume in-8° crown of 600 pages.

Subscribers will be notified when the volume appears, which will be sent to them by registered post immediately on receipt of payment.

All correspondence, cheques, money-orders should be addressed to :

Miss SYLVIA BEACH

"SHAKESPEARE AND COMPANY"

8, RUE DUPUYTREN, PARIS — VI

● **PRE-PUBLICITY MATERIAL FOR *ULYSSES*,** showing a wide spectrum of critical opinion.

To Harriet Weaver
in token of gratitude
James Joyce

Paris
13 February 1922

I give this first copy of Ulysses to
the National Library of Ireland
after thirty years
Harriet Weaver.

Oxford
S. Patrick's Day 1952

● **WEAVER INSCRIPTION.**
Joyce inscribed this first copy of
the first edition of *Ulysses* to his
patron Harriet Weaver, 'in
token of gratitude'; in 1952 she
donated it to the National
Library of Ireland.

● **FORD MADOX FORD, JAMES JOYCE,**
EZRA POUND AND JOHN QUINN, Paris,
1923. Ford's magazine, *Transatlantic Review*,
printed the first fragment of 'Work in
progress' (which ultimately became
Finnegans wake) in the following year.

Courtesy of the Poetry/Rare Books Collection,
University Libraries, State University of New York at
Buffalo

● **ADRIENNE MONNIER
(1892–1955),** in her bookshop,
La Maison des Amis des Livres,
on the Rue de l'Odéon in Paris.
Monnier brought out the French
translation of *Ulysses* in 1929,
five years after it was begun.

● **VALERY LARBAUD
(1881–1957),** the French critic
who hailed *Ulysses* as a
masterpiece and was one of the
translators who worked on the
French version, *Ulysse*, for
Adrienne Monnier.

Courtesy of the University of Tulsa,
Department of Special Collections

● **JAMES JOYCE WITH
CLOVIS MONNIER,** father of
Adrienne Monnier, who
published the French
translation of *Ulysses*.

● **PADRAIC COLUM (1881–1972),** who knew Joyce as a young
man in Dublin. Colum and his wife Mary became very friendly with
Joyce in later years; the Colums wrote the memoir *Our friend James
Joyce* together.

● CONSTANTINE CURRAN AND NORA AND JAMES JOYCE, c. 1935.

● JOYCE WITH EUGENE JOLAS, who was the editor of *Transition* magazine with his wife Maria. Instalments of 'Work in progress' appeared in the magazine in 1927.

Courtesy of the Zurich James Joyce Foundation

● PAUL LÉON WITH JOYCE'S IRISH FRIEND CONSTANTINE CURRAN. Curran attended University College with Joyce, and the two remained lifelong friends.

Can You any longer resist the Call?

YOUR KING AND COUNTRY NEED YOU.

A CALL TO ARMS.

An addition of 100,000 men to His Majesty's Regular Army is immediately necessary in the present grave National Emergency.

Lord Kitchener is confident that this appeal will be at once responded to by all those who have the safety of our Empire at heart.

TERMS OF SERVICE.

General Service for a period of 3 years or until the war is concluded.

Age of Enlistment between 19 and 30.

HOW TO JOIN.

Full information can be obtained a[t] any Post Office in the Kingdom or at an[y] Military depot.

GOD SAVE THE KING.

Printed for H.M. Stationery Office by W. P. GRIFFITH & SONS LTD., London, [

[70] W2462/2139 1000m 8/14

● **REDMOND'S ADVICE.**
Leaflet attacking the advice of
John Redmond, leader of the
Irish Parliamentary Party, that
Irishmen should join the British
army and fight in World War I,
for the freedom of small
nations.

● **RECRUITING MATERIAL
FROM WORLD WAR I.** 'Can
you any longer resist the call?',
linking iconic images of
Irishness to the war effort, was
issued by the Department of
Recruiting for Ireland.

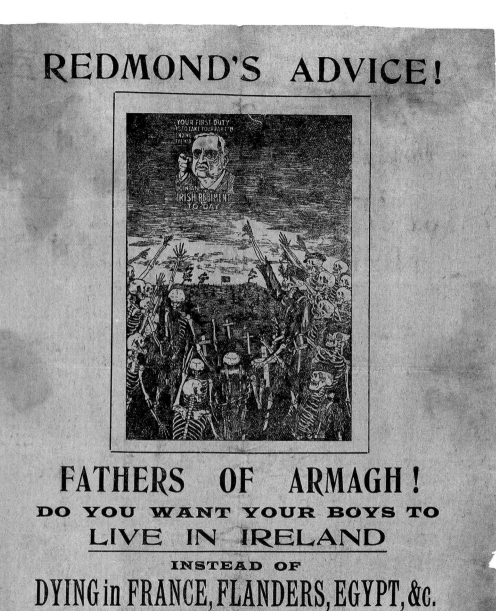

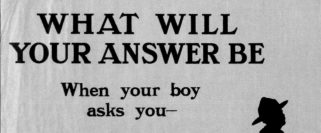

● '"I'LL GO TOO!" The real Irish spirit.' Poster issued by the Central Council for Recruiting in Ireland, 1915.

● 'WHAT WILL YOUR ANSWER BE?'. Poster for the recruitment effort in Ireland, 1914–15. Some 49,000 Irish recruits were to lose their lives before the conflict ended in 1918.

● 'WAR!! England, Germany and Ireland'. Anti-recruitment leaflet, urging Irishmen not to join the British war effort.

● 'THE CONSCRIPTS' CHORUS'. Leaflet attacking the policies of the British prime minister, David Lloyd George, during World War I.

WAR!!

ENGLAND, GERMANY AND IRELAND.

The mighty British Empire is on the verge of destruction. "The hand of the Lord hath touched her." The English live in daily terror of Germany. War between England and Germany is at hand. England's cowardly and degenerate population won't make soldiers: not so the Germans. They are trained and ready.

WHAT WILL ENGLAND DO?

She'll get Irish Fools to join her Army and Navy, send them to fight and die for her Empire. England has never fought her own battles. Irish traitors have ever been the backbone of her Army and Navy. How has she rewarded them? When they are no longer able to fight she flings them back to Ireland, reeking with foul filthy diseases to die in the workhouses.

WHY SHOULD YOU FIGHT FOR ENGLAND?

Is it in gratitude for the Priest-hunters and the rack of the Penal days! The Gibbet! The Pitch Cap! The Half-hangings and all the Horrors of '98?

Is it in gratitude for the Famine when One Million of our people were slowly starved to death, and Christian England thanking God that the Celts were going, going with a vengeance?

Is it in gratitude for the blazing homesteads and the people half-naked and starved to death by the roadside?

STAND ASIDE

and have your revenge. Without Ireland's help England will go down before Germany as she would have gone down before the Boers had not the Irish fought her battle in South Africa. The English know this and they have offered us a bribe and call it

HOME RULE.

It is not yet law, but believing us to be a nation of fools she wants payment in advance, and has sent her warships to our coasts to entrap young Irishmen.

THE VIGILANCE COMMITTEE

feels bound to issue this solemn warning to young Irishmen against joining the English Army or Navy—for your own sake, as well as for your country's sake. You denounce as traitors the men who sold their votes to pass the Union. You denounce Judas who sold Christ, but generations yet unborn will curse YOU who now join England's Army or Navy. Aye, will curse not alone the dupes who join, but also those who neglect to aid the VIGILANCE COMMITTEE in their crusade against the most Immoral Army and Navy in the world.

The Conscripts' Chorus.

AN EXECRATION OF LLOYD GEORGE.

LLOYD GEORGE, no doubt, when his life ebbs out,
Will ride in a flaming chariot,
And will sit in state on a red-hot plate,
'Twixt the Devil and Judas Iscariot.
Ananias that day to Old Nick will say:
My precedence here now fails,
So move me up higher, away from the fire,
And make room for the Lawyer from Wales.

● **PORTRAIT OF STEPHEN GWYNN, MP,** by Walter Osborne, recovered from the ruins of the Royal Irish Academy after the Easter rebellion of 1916. In 1903, during his brief career as a book reviewer for the *Daily Express,* Joyce had reviewed Gwynn's *Today and tomorrow in Ireland.*

● **'AFTER THE BOMBARDMENT:** The holocaust of Ireland's greatest thoroughfare, Friday morning, 29th April, 1916'. During the Easter rebellion of 1916, O'Connell (then Sackville) Street was shelled and several of the buildings destroyed.

F. 26.

VOTER—THINK

If you do so you WILL give Sinn Fein a chance.

DON'T BE INFLUENCED

By a subsidised sham National Press, by Placemen, Job Cadgers, or the Shivery-Shakers—who ape gentility by having the same opinions as the " Cromwellian " Gentry.

IRELAND IS YOUR COUNTRY

DON'T BE ASHAMED

To advocate for it what the world is advocating for every other Small Nation. Sinn Fein is working for Freedom. Come along and help the weak.

BE A MAN FOR IRELAND'S SAKE.

For your own sake. Think of the blessedness of Freedom.

" For the Glory of God and the Honour of Ireland " our best have died. Many are in English prisons. We have you to help.

DO SO—

VOTE RIGHT.

ARTHUR GRIFFITH MICHAEL COLLINS

1/- net.

● **COVER OF *ARTHUR GRIFFITH, MICHAEL COLLINS,*** illustrated by Harry Clarke, 1922. Both Griffith and Collins, supporters of the Anglo-Irish Treaty of 1921, died shortly after the outbreak of the Civil War in Ireland in June 1922, Griffith of a brain haemorrhage and Collins in an ambush. In *Ulysses* Griffith, 'the coming man', is frequently referred to.

● **'VOTER—THINK'.** Political leaflet for the Sinn Féin party, c. 1918, advocating Irish nationhood.

ULYSSES

● **THE LITTLE REVIEW, SEPTEMBER 1920.** Episodes of *Ulysses* appeared in the magazine between 1918 and 1920, with 'Oxen of the Sun' the last episode to appear. The New York Society for the Suppression of Vice lodged an official complaint against the work, and in February of 1921 the editors of *The Little Review* were prosecuted and fined for publishing the episodes of *Ulysses*.

● *ULYSSES* ANNOUNCEMENT. A slightly premature announcement of the forthcoming publication of *Ulysses* in the autumn of 1921. The book was not published until February 1922.

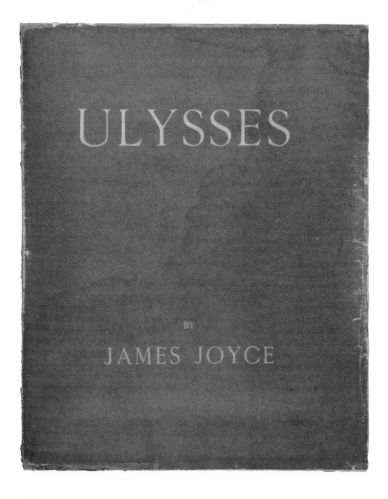

ULYSSES

BY

JAMES JOYCE

THIS EDITION IS LIMITED TO 1000 COPIES :
100 COPIES (SIGNED) ON DUTCH
HANDMADE PAPER NUMBERED FROM
1 TO 100 ; 150 COPIES ON VERGÉ
- D'ARCHES NUMBERED FROM 101 TO 250 ;
750 COPIES ON HANDMADE PAPER
NUMBERED FROM 251 TO 1000.

N° UNNUMBERED PRESS COPY

● **FIRST EDITION** of *Ulysses* by
James Joyce. The colours of the
cover were chosen to
correspond with those of the
Greek flag.

● **DETAIL FROM A PRESS
COPY OF *ULYSSES*** sent to the
National Library of Ireland by
the publisher Sylvia Beach,
proprietor of Shakespeare and
Company, on the instructions of
James Joyce.

● **THREE COPIES OF THE FIRST EDITION** of *Ulysses*
in the National Library of Ireland.

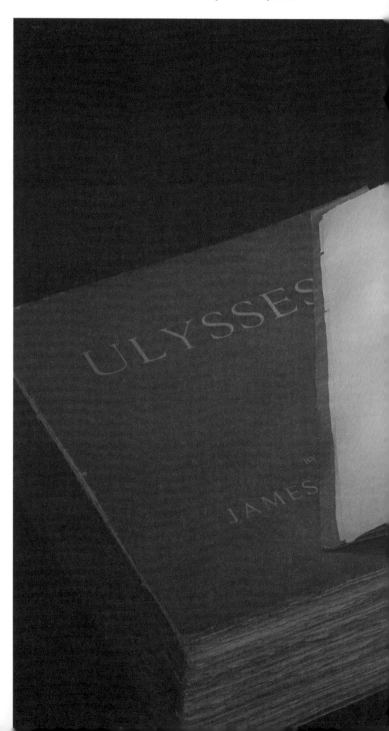

BY THE SAME WRITER
CHAMBER MUSIC
DUBLINERS
A PORTRAIT OF THE ARTIST AS A YOUNG MAN
EXILES
THE EGOIST PRESS
LONDON
ULYSSES
by
JAMES JOYCE
PRESS COPY
SHAKESPEARE AND COMPANY
12, Rue de l'Odéon, 12
PARIS
1922
JOYCE

● **GRAFTON STREET, DUBLIN,** looking toward O'Connell Street. Leopold Bloom strolls through the city centre in the eighth episode, 'Lestrygonians', moving from O'Connell (then Sackville) Street to the fashionable shopping district of Grafton Street.

● **BARNEY KIERNAN'S PUB,** Little Britain Street, where the twelfth episode of *Ulysses*, 'Cyclops', takes place.

O'Connell Bridge and Sackville Street, Dublin

● **SACKVILLE STREET.** A view of Sackville (O'Connell) Street, looking towards Nelson's Pillar. Much of the action of the seventh episode of *Ulysses*, 'Aeolus' takes place on the premises of the *Freeman's Journal* newspaper, off Sackville Street on Prince's Street.

● **GIBRALTAR.** Watercolour of Gibraltar by Jeanie Conan, 1888. In *Ulysses* Molly Bloom lived in Gibraltar during the 1870s and 1880s.

Gibraltar

Galleries cut in the

● **ECCLES STREET**. Detail of a knocker on a Georgian door, Eccles Street, photographed by Eleanor Wiltshire. In *Ulysses* the Blooms are living at No. 7, Eccles Street.

● *ULYSSES*, **FIRST EDITION**, fourth printing, 1924. The fourth, fifth and sixth printings of *Ulysses* for Shakespeare and Company were issued on inexpensive paper and bound in white paper covers with the title and author printed in blue.

Europe Pt. Gibraltar

● **GIBRALTAR.** Watercolour of
Gibraltar by Jeanie Conan, 1888.
During her reminiscences in
'Penelope', the final episode of
Ulysses, Molly Bloom recalls growing
up on the island of Gibraltar.

Left cover:

The FIRST CHAPTER of ULYSSES By JAMES JOYCE

TWO WORLDS MONTHLY

Devoted to the Increase of the Gaiety of Nations

Partial Contents of
VOLUME ONE   NUMBER ONE

First instalment of ULYSSES....James Joyce

James Joyce................Arthur Symons

A Dose of Salts................Heinrich Heine

Twelve Great Passions: Fra Filippo Lippi................J. A. Brendon

The Fate of the Baron......Arthur Schnitzler

The Shadow in the Rose Garden................D. H. Lawrence

A Literary Holiday: Prologue....Samuel Roth

The Two Nude Virgins......A. E. Coppard

TWO WORLDS PUBLISHING COMPANY
500 FIFTH AVE., Suite 405-8, NEW YORK

Edited by Samuel Roth

PRICE FIFTY CENTS

Right cover:

MR. ROTH HALED INTO COURT

TWO WORLDS MONTHLY

Devoted to the Increase of the Gaiety of Nations

Edited by Samuel Roth

PRICE FIFTY CENTS

ULYSSES (9th Instalment)   APRIL 1927   JOAN LA ROMEE by FRANK   HARRIS

● TWO ISSUES OF THE
AMERICAN PERIODICAL
TWO WORLDS MONTHLY,
run by Samuel Roth. It
published instalments of a
pirated version of *Ulysses,*
beginning in July 1926.

● PROTEST AGAINST THE
ROTH PIRACY OF *ULYSSES,*
February 1927, signed by 167
eminent figures, including
Albert Einstein, T.S. Eliot, Ernest
Hemingway and W.B. Yeats.

Paris, 2nd February 1927.

It is a matter of common knowledge that the *Ulysses* of Mr. James Joyce is being republished in the United States, in a magazine edited by Samuel Roth, and that this republication is being made without authorization by Mr. Joyce; without payment to Mr. Joyce and with alterations which seriously corrupt the text. This appropriation and mutilation of Mr. Joyce's property is made under colour of legal protection in that the *Ulysses* which is published in France and which has been excluded from the mails in the United States is not protected by copyright in the United States. The question of justification of that exclusion is not now in issue ; similar decisions have been made by government officials with reference to works of art before this. The question in issue is whether the public (including the editors and publishers to whom his advertisements are offered) will encourage Mr. Samuel Roth to take advantage of the resultant legal difficulty of the author to deprive him of his property and to mutilate the creation of his art. The undersigned protest against Mr. Roth's conduct in republishing *Ulysses* and appeal to the American public in the name of that security of works of the intellect and the imagination without which art cannot live, to oppose to Mr. Roth's enterprise the full power of honorable and fair opinion.

LASCELLES ABERCROMBIE.
RICHARD ALDINGTON.
SHERWOOD ANDERSON.
RENÉ ARCOS.
M. ARCYBACHEFF.
EBBA ATTERBOM.
AZORIN, *Président de l'Académie Espagnole.*
C. DU BAISSAURAY.
LÉON BAZALGETTE.
JACINTO BENAVENTE.
SILVIO BENCO.
JULIEN BENDA.
ARNOLD BENNETT.
JACQUES BENOIST-MÉCHIN.
KONRAD BERCOVICI.
J. D. BERESFORD.
RUDOLF BINDING.
MASSIMO BONTEMPELLI.
JEAN DE BOSSCHÈRE.
IVAN BOUNINE, *de l'Académie Russe.*
ROBERT BRIDGES.
EUGÈNE BRIEUX, *de l'Académie Française.*
BRYHER.
OLAF BULL.
MARY BUTTS.
LOUIS CAZAMIAN.
JACQUES CHENEVIÈRE.
ABEL CHEVALLEY.
MAURICE CONSTANTIN-WÉYER.
ALBERT CRÉMIEUX.
BENJAMIN CRÉMIEUX.
BENEDETTO CROCE.
ERNST ROBERT CURTIUS.
FRANCIS DICKIE.
H. D.
NORMAN DOUGLAS.
CHARLES DU BOS.
GEORGES DUHAMEL.
ÉDOUARD DUJARDIN.
LUC DURTAIN.
ALBERT EINSTEIN.
T. S. ELIOT.
HAVELOCK ELLIS.
ÉDOUARD ESTAUNIÉ, *de l'Académie française.*
LÉON-PAUL FARGUE.
E. M. FORSTER.
FRANÇOIS FOSCA.
GASTON GALLIMARD.
JOHN GALSWORTHY.
EDWARD GARNETT.
GIOVANNI GENTILE.
PHILIP GIBBS.
ANDRÉ GIDE.
BERNARD GILBERT.

IVAN GOLL.
RAMON GOMEZ DE LA SERNA.
CORA GORDON.
JAN GORDON.
GEORG GOYERT.
ALICE S. GREEN.
JULIAN GREEN.
AUGUSTA GREGORY.
DANIEL HALÉVY.
KNUT HAMSUN.
JANE HARRISON.
H. LIVINGSTON HARTLEY.
ERNEST HEMINGWAY.
YRJÖ HIRN.
HUGO VON HOFMANNSTHAL.
SISLEY HUDDLESTON.
STEPHEN HUDSON.
GEORGE F. HUMMEL.
BAMPTON HUNT.
BRAVIG IMBS.
HOLBROOK JACKSON.
EDMOND JALOUX.
STORM JAMESON.
JUAN RAMON JIMENEZ.
EUGÈNE JOLAS.
HENRY FESTING JONES.
GEORG KAISER.
HERMANN KEYSERLING.
MANUEL KOMROFF.
A. KOUPRINE.
RENÉ LALOU.
PIERRE DE LANUX.
VALERY LARBAUD.
D. H. LAWRENCE.
FRÉDÉRIC LEFÈVRE.
ÉMILE LEGOUIS.
WYNDHAM LEWIS.
LUDWIG LEWISOHN.
VICTOR LLONA.
MINA LOY.
ARCHIBALD MACLEISH.
BRINSLEY MACNAMARA.
MAURICE MAETERLINCK.
THOMAS MANN.
ANTONIO MARICHALAR.
MAURICE MARTIN DU GARD.
DORA MARSDEN.
JOHN MASEFIELD.
W. SOMERSET MAUGHAM.
ANDRÉ MAUROIS.
D. MEREJKOWSKY.
RÉGIS MICHAUD.
GABRIEL MIRÓ.
HOPE MIRRLEES.
T. STURGE MOORE.
PAUL MORAND.
AUGUSTE MOREL.
ARTHUR MOSS.

J. MIDDLETON MURRY.
SEAN O'CASEY.
LIAM O'FLAHERTY.
JOSÉ ORTEGA Y GASSET.
SEUMAS O'SULLIVAN.
ELLIOT H. PAUL.
JEAN PAULHAN.
ARTHUR PINERO.
LUIGI PIRANDELLO.
JEAN PRÉVOST.
MARCEL PRÉVOST, *de l'Académie Française.*
C. F. RAMUZ.
ALFONSO REYES.
ERNEST RHYS.
ELMER E. RICE.
DOROTHY RICHARDSON.
JACQUES ROBERTFRANCE.
LENNOX ROBINSON.
JOHN RODKER.
ROMAIN ROLLAND.
JULES ROMAINS.
BERTRAND RUSSELL.
GEORGE W. RUSSELL « A. E. ».
LUDMILLA SAVITZKY.
JEAN SCHLUMBERGER.
MAY SINCLAIR.
W. L. SMYSER.
E. Œ. SOMERVILLE.
PHILIPPE SOUPAULT.
ANDRÉ SPIRE.
TH. STEPHANIDES.
JAMES STEPHENS.
ANDRÉ SUARES.
ITALO SVEVO.
FRANK SWINNERTON.
ARTHUR SYMONS.
MARCEL THIÉBAUT.
VIRGIL THOMSON.
ROBERT DE TRAZ.
C. R. TREVELYAN.
MIGUEL DE UNAMUNO.
LAURENCE VAIL.
PAUL VALÉRY, *de l'Académie Française.*
FERNAND VANDÉREM.
FRITZ VANDERPYL.
FRANCIS VIÉLÉ-GRIFFIN.
HUGH WALPOLE.
JACOB WASSERMANN.
H. G. WELLS.
REBECCA WEST.
ANNA WICKHAM.
THORNTON WILDER.
ROBERT WOLF.
VIRGINIA WOOLF.
W. B. YEATS.

JAMES JOYCE · Photo d'amateur

ULYSSE

PAR
JAMES JOYCE

TRADUCTION FRANÇAISE INTÉGRALE PAR
MM. AUGUSTE MOREL et STUART-GILBERT
entièrement revue par
M. VALERY LARBAUD
avec la collaboration de l'AUTEUR.

POUR PARAITRE EN JANVIER 1929
à LA MAISON DES AMIS DES LIVRES
— Adrienne Monnier —
7, RUE DE L'ODÉON — PARIS, VIᵉ

"ULYSSES"
by James Joyce

The book that has been discussed more than any other in recent years. Erotic literature at its best. Every connoisseur should have read Ulysses, and as the edition is strictly limited, opportunities to obtain a copy are daily getting scarcer. Privately printed.

Price................. $ **5.-** or £ **1/-**

LADY CHATTERLEY'S LOVER
by D. H. Lawrence

A masterpiece by the celebrated author. Not afraid of mincing words or situations, Lawrence's novel ranks among the star books which will become classics of love and eroticsm. Repeatedly banned, this is the only complete and unexpurgated edition obtainable to-day. Privately printed.

Price................. $ **3.-** or **12/-**
— 24 —

● **ANNOUNCEMENT OF THE FRENCH TRANSLATION** of *Ulysses*, published by La Maison des Amis des Livres in 1929.

THE VICES OF WOMEN
MODERN VICES OF WOMAN AND FEMININE CONFIDENCES
The fervent passion of young grils seized by a saphic aberration.
This book disclose a perverse hand bewildering sensuality which makes its lecture highly attractive.
Price. . . . .   **\$ 5.-** or £ **I/-**

THE MONUMENTAL DECISION OF THE
UNITED STATES DISTRICT COURT
RENDERED DECEMBER 6, 1933, BY HON.
JOHN M. WOOLSEY LIFTING THE BAN ON
"ULYSSES."

UNITED STATES DISTRICT COURT
SOUTHERN DISTRICT OF NEW YORK

United States of America, *Libelant*		
v.		OPINION
One Book called "Ulysses" Random House, Inc., *Claimant*		A. 110-59

On cross motions for a decree in a libel of confiscation, supplemented by a stipulation—hereinafter described—brought by the United States against the book "Ulysses" by James Joyce, under Section 305 of the Tariff Act of 1930, Title 19 United States Code, Section 1305, on the ground that the book is obscene within the meaning of that Section, and, hence, is not importable into the United States, but is subject to seizure, forfeiture and confiscation and destruction.

United States Attorney—by Samuel C. Coleman, Esq., and Nicholas Atlas, Esq., of counsel—for the United States, in support of motion for a decree of forfeiture, and in opposition to motion for a decree dismissing the libel.

Messrs. Greenbaum, Wolff & Ernst,—by Morris L. Ernst, Esq., and Alexander Lindey, Esq., of counsel—attorneys for claimant Random House, Inc., in support of motion for a decree dismissing the libel, and in opposition to motion for a decree of forfeiture.

[ix]

● *ULYSSES* AS EROTIC LITERATURE. Entry for *Ulysses* in a list of pornographic literature entitled 'Curious books'.

● WOOLSEY DECISION. Text of the decision by Justice Woolsey, 1933, overturning the ban on *Ulysses* in the United States.

● **USA VS *ULYSSES*.** Text of the Woolsey judgement, which overturned the US ban on *Ulysses* in 1933.

THE
MODERN LIBRARY

A series of 214 outstanding modern books, well printed and handsomely bound, designed to sell for 95 cents a copy.

Two of James Joyce's best-known books are available in the Modern Library series. They are "DUBLINERS" (volume #124) and "A PORTRAIT OF THE ARTIST AS A YOUNG MAN" (volume #145).

Other authors represented in the Modern Library include:

ERNEST HEMINGWAY
GERTRUDE STEIN
EUGENE O'NEILL
THOMAS MANN
WILLIAM FAULKNER
VIRGINIA WOOLF
ERSKINE CALDWELL
KATHERINE MANSFIELD
D. H. LAWRENCE

Bennett A. Cerf and Donald S. Klopfer, directors of Random House, are also the publishers of The Modern Library. They will be pleased to mail a complete list of titles on request.

THE MODERN LIBRARY
20 E. 57TH ST., NEW YORK

A few of the outstanding books published by

RANDOM HOUSE

THE BROTHERS KARAMAZOV
A beautiful new edition of Dostoyevsky's masterpiece, in Constance Garnett's unabridged translation, with 26 illustrations by Boardman Robinson. $3.50

THE ROCKWELL KENT MOBY DICK
Herman Melville's classic in its proper setting at last, with over 200 illustrations by Rockwell Kent. $3.50

PLAYS AND POEMS OF W. S. GILBERT
The Gilbert and Sullivan operas complete, and all the Bab Ballads. With 200 illustrations by the author, and a long introduction by Deems Taylor. $3.50

THE ROMANCE OF LEONARDO DA VINCI
Merejkowski's great novel in an unabridged translation by Bernard Guerney. Illustrated. $5.00

THE WRITINGS OF WILLIAM BLAKE, JOHN DONNE, SAMUEL COLERIDGE, AND WILLIAM HAZLITT
These volumes, produced in partnership with the Nonesuch Press in London, are designed to satisfy the exacting scholar as well as the discriminating collector. Each volume, $3.50

RANDOM HOUSE
is the publisher of all of the books of EUGENE O'NEILL and ROBINSON JEFFERS and the exclusive distributor in America of the books of the NONESUCH PRESS.

● **RANDOM HOUSE *ULYSSES* EDITION.** Jacket of the first authorised American edition of *Ulysses*, published by Random House in 1934. This edition, unfortunately (and unwittingly), was based on the slipshod and corrupt piracy published by Samuel Roth in 1929.

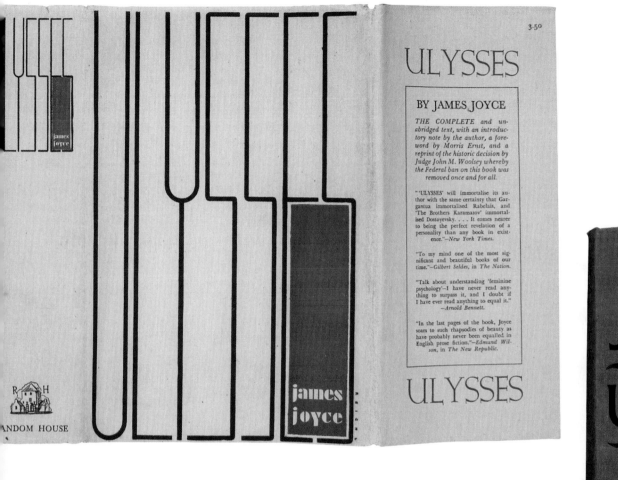

3.50

ULYSSES

BY JAMES JOYCE

THE COMPLETE and un-
abridged text, with an introduc-
tory note by the author, a fore-
word by Morris Ernst, and a
reprint of the historic decision by
Judge John M. Woolsey whereby
the Federal ban on this book was
removed once and for all.

"'ULYSSES' will immortalise its author with the same certainty that Gar-
gantua immortalised Rabelais, and
'The Brothers Karamazov' immortalised Dostoyevsky. . . . It comes nearer
to being the perfect revelation of a
personality than any book in exist-
ence."—*New York Times.*

"To my mind one of the most significant and beautiful books of our
time."—*Gilbert Seldes, in The Nation.*

"Talk about understanding 'feminine
psychology'—I have never read anything to surpass it, and I doubt if
I have ever read anything to equal it."
—*Arnold Bennett.*

"In the last pages of the book, Joyce
soars to such rhapsodies of beauty as
have probably never been equalled in
English prose fiction."—*Edmund Wil-
son, in The New Republic.*

ULYSSES

● *JAMES JOYCE'S ULYSSES:*
a study by Stuart Gilbert,
published in 1930, the first
book-length study of the novel.

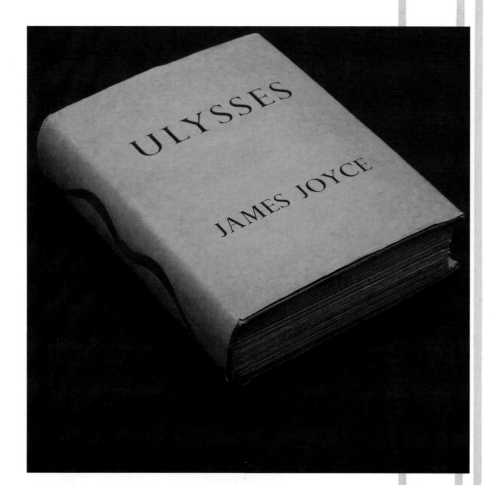

● **A SMALL SAMPLE OF THE MANY DIFFERENT EDITIONS OF** *ULYSSES,* including the 1934 Random House edition (back row, far left) and the Limited Editions Club edition of 1935 (back row, far right), featuring illustrations by Henri Matisse.

● **THE 1936 BODLEY HEAD EDITION OF** *ULYSSES,* the first edition of the novel to be published in England, featuring the bow of Ulysses designed by Eric Gill.

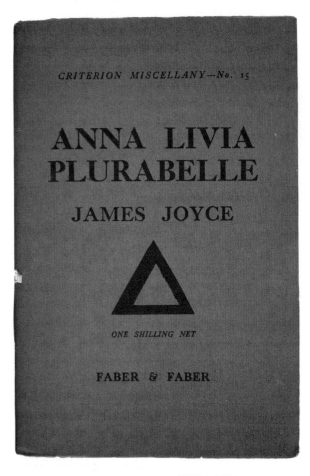

CRITERION MISCELLANY—No. 15

ANNA LIVIA PLURABELLE

JAMES JOYCE

ONE SHILLING NET

FABER & FABER

OUR EXAGMINATION
ROUND HIS FACTIFICATION
FOR INCAMINATION
OF "WORK IN PROGRESS"

by

Samuel Beckett, Marcel Brion, Frank Budgen, Stuart Gilbert, Eugene Jolas, Victor Llona, Robert McAlmon, Thomas McGreevy, Elliot Paul, John Rodker, Robert Sage, William Carlos Williams

A Survey of James Joyce's
"WORK IN PROGRESS" PARTS 1 and 3
from twelve different angles

(" DANTE, BRUNO, VICO AND JOYCE ", " WORK IN PROGRESS AND OLD NORSE POETRY ", " THE TREATMENT OF PLOT ", " AN IRISH WORD BALLET ", etc.)

PRICE : 24 FRANCS

SHAKESPEARE AND COMPANY
SYLVIA BEACH
12, RUE DE L'ODÉON, 12
PARIS · VI*

● 'ANNA LIVIA PLURABELLE', 1930, a fragment of 'Work in progress' (which would eventually become *Finnegans wake*).

● ANNOUNCEMENT OF THE PUBLICATION OF *OUR EXAGMINATION ROUND HIS FACTIFICATION FOR INCAMINATION OF 'WORK IN PROGRESS'*, a book of essays brought out by Shakespeare and Company to help elucidate 'Work in progress'.

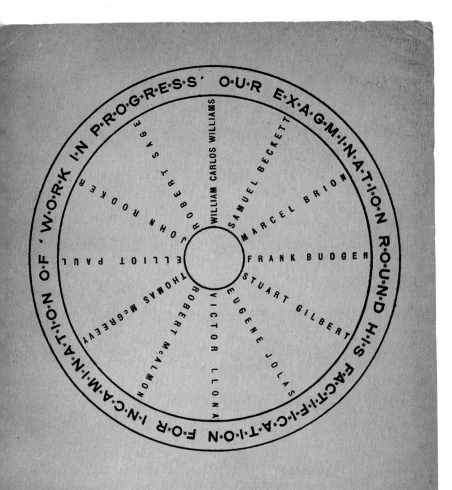

'WORK IN PROGRESS' OUR EXAGMINATION ROUND HIS FACTIFICATION FOR INCAMINATION OF

WILLIAM CARLOS WILLIAMS
ROBERT SAGE
JOHN ROOKER
ELLIOT PAUL
THOMAS McGREEVY
ROBERT McALMON
VICTOR LLONA
EUGENE JOLAS
STUART GILBERT
FRANK BUDGEN
MARCEL BRION
SAMUEL BECKETT

SHAKESPEARE AND COMPANY
12, RUE DE L'ODÉON, PARIS
MCMXXIX

Tales Told of
Shem and Shaun

Three Fragments from
Work in Progress

by

JAMES JOYCE

THE BLACK SUN PRESS
RUE CARDINALE
PARIS
MCMXXIX

● *OUR EXAGMINATION ROUND HIS FACTIFICATION FOR INCAMINATION OF 'WORK IN PROGRESS'*, 1929, containing essays by, among others, Samuel Beckett.

● **'TALES TOLD OF SHEM AND SHAUN', 1929,** a fragment of 'Work in progress'. Harry and Caresse Crosby's Black Sun Press, which published this edition, brought together a diverse community of artists.

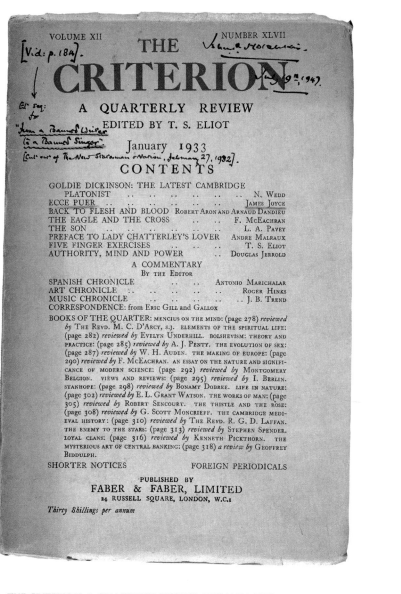

VOLUME XII   NUMBER XLVII

THE
CRITERION

A QUARTERLY REVIEW
EDITED BY T. S. ELIOT

January 1933

CONTENTS

PUBLISHED BY
FABER & FABER, LIMITED
24 RUSSELL SQUARE, LONDON, W.C.1

Thirty Shillings per annum

THE MIME OF MICK, NICK
AND THE MAGGIES

JAMES   JOYCE

● *THE CRITERION: A QUARTERLY REVIEW*, JANUARY 1933,
which published the poem *Ecce puer*, written by Joyce on the birth
of his only grandchild, Stephen.

● 'THE MIME OF MICK, NICK
AND THE MAGGIES', 1934, a
fragment of 'Work in progress',
with an initial letter, tailpiece
and cover designed by Lucia
Joyce.

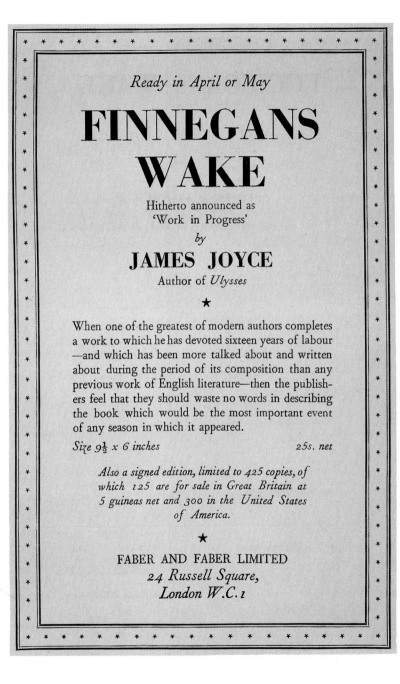

Ready in April or May

FINNEGANS WAKE

Hitherto announced as
'Work in Progress'

by

JAMES JOYCE

Author of *Ulysses*

★

When one of the greatest of modern authors completes
a work to which he has devoted sixteen years of labour
—and which has been more talked about and written
about during the period of its composition than any
previous work of English literature—then the publishers feel that they should waste no words in describing
the book which would be the most important event
of any season in which it appeared.

Size 9½ x 6 inches   *25s. net*

*Also a signed edition, limited to 425 copies, of
which 125 are for sale in Great Britain at
5 guineas net and 300 in the United States
of America.*

★

FABER AND FABER LIMITED
*24 Russell Square,
London W.C.1*

● ANNOUNCEMENT OF THE
PUBLICATION OF
FINNEGANS WAKE, the name
under which 'Work in progress'
was eventually published by
Faber and Faber in 1939.

● *FINNEGANS WAKE,*
1939.

● **CORRECTIONS OF
MISPRINTS IN
FINNEGANS WAKE,
1945.** Joyce worked with
Paul Léon over the
summer of 1940 to
compile this list. By
January of the following
year, James Joyce had
died in Zurich,
Switzerland, aged 58.

See Slocum 48

Corrections of Misprints in
FINNEGANS WAKE
BY JAMES JOYCE

As Prepared by the Author after
Publication of the First Edition

PUBLISHED 1945 BY
THE VIKING PRESS · NEW YORK
for distribution to purchasers of
FINNEGANS WAKE

GOTHAM BOOK MART
51 WEST 47th STREET
NEW YORK, N. Y.

● **CELEBRATIONS OF THE
FIFTIETH ANNIVERSARY OF
BLOOMSDAY,** photographed by
Eleanor Wiltshire. On 16 June 1954 a
group of Irish writers gathered to
celebrate the fiftieth anniversary of
Bloomsday.

BLOOMSDAY

● **FIFTIETH-ANNIVERSARY BLOOMSDAY CELEBRATIONS,** photographed by Eleanor Wiltshire. The Irish writers commemorating James Joyce in Davy Byrne's pub included Patrick Kavanagh (reading) and Flann O'Brien (on Kavanagh's left).